Domestic Violence Death Reviews and Femicide

Domestic Violence Death Reviews and Femicide

Theory, Research, Practice, Policy

Desmond Ellis

ROWMAN & LITTLEFIELD
Lanham • Boulder • New York • London

Rowman & Littlefield
Bloomsbury Publishing Inc, 1385 Broadway, New York, NY 10018, USA
Bloomsbury Publishing Plc, 50 Bedford Square, London, WC1B 3DP, UK
Bloomsbury Publishing Ireland, 29 Earlsfort Terrace, Dublin 2, D02 AY28, Ireland
www.rowman.com

British Library Cataloguing in Publication Information available

Library of Congress Cataloging-in-Publication Data available
ISBN: 978-1-5381-9725-7 (cloth)
ISBN: 978-1-5381-9726-4 (paperback)
ISBN: 978-1-5381-9727-1 (electronic)

For product safety related questions contact productsafety@bloomsbury.com.

∞™ The paper used in this publication meets the minimum requirements of
American National Standard for Information Sciences—Permanence of Paper for
Printed Library Materials, ANSI/NISO Z39.48-1992.

Dedicated to family members, relatives, friends, neighbors, and coworkers who in their everyday lives attempt to prevent gender-based violence against women.

Contents

Introduction

This book is about an epidemic of coercively controlling conduct, nonfatal (e.g., attempted strangulation), and fatal violence (femicide) perpetrated by males against female intimate partners, and the attempts made by domestic violence death reviews (DVDRs) to end it. More specifically, this book describes how DVDRs attempt to end the epidemic by making appropriate recommendations to community-based organizations and agencies in the United States, Canada, and the United Kingdom whose mandates include promoting the safety of women.

An epidemic becomes a social issue when it becomes a social problem about which the public feels something should be done. But what does "epidemic" mean? In the public health literature, an epidemic is defined as the widespread occurrence of public-health-related conduct causing fatal and nonfatal harm at a particular time and place. Coercively controlling conduct and nonfatal violence by male partners are potent predictors of femicide. In this book, an epidemic is defined as the high rate at which women in these three countries were and are being coercively controlled, injured, and killed by their male partners since 1994 when the first FRT was established in Santa Clara (Druscovich & Caspari, 2023; Hayes, 2023; Long et al., 2017; United Nations, 2022).

Although femicide is relatively rare, in the present context it represents the most visible tip of an iceberg consisting of harms intentionally inflicted on thousands of females by their male intimate partners. So, the iceberg is an epidemic that includes both predictors of femicide—coercively controlling conduct and nonfatal male partner violence—and femicides. In this iceberg, femicides at the tip represent a boulder larger

1

than one made by its predictors, dropped in a pond that creates far larger ripples of sadness and suffering for loved ones. Evidence supporting this conclusion follows.

For every 100 women murdered by a male partner, attempts are made to murder as many as 500 more (Dobson, 2002). Other adverse health effects of femicide include suicides by perpetrators and survivors of attempted homicides (Kafka et al., 2022), psychological problems such as posttraumatic stress disorder (PTSD), depression, guilt, anxiety, and trauma experienced by surviving family members (Canadian Parents of Murdered Children, 2020; Connolly & Gordon, 2015; Zinov et al., 2009), homelessness among female partners experiencing precursors of femicide such as coercive control tactics and separation (Ali, 2023), intergenerational trauma experienced by children of perpetrators and victims (Canadian Parents of Murdered Children, 2020), victim blaming of relatives and survivors of murder by investigating police officers (Woods, 2023), and increases in a sense of insecurity in the local communities and the wider society in which femicides occur (UNODC, 2022; World Health Organization, 2020).

Traditionally, the social issue of violence against women generally, and femicides in particular, resulted in a criminal justice system response aimed at deterring potential perpetrators of femicide (Shepherd, 2001). Domestic homicide death reviews represented a wider, innovative, alternative socio-legal response to this social issue.

For readers who may not be familiar with DVDRs, a brief description of the start and end points of an average DVDR workday in Ontario, Canada, follows: a person(s) who dies of unnatural causes is discovered; police and coroners arrive at the scene; the death is reported to the Office of the Chief Coroner; deaths classified as domestic violence homicides are referred to the domestic violence death reviews committee (DVDRC) whose members—sworn to secrecy—review them, and make recommendations aimed at preventing them to appropriate community-based organizations and agencies. The kinds of homicide cases the DVDRC reviews include the case of a husband who deliberately ran over his wife with his car when she told him she was leaving him, and a wife who stabbed her drunken lover to death during an argument when he threatened to kill her and her two children. All the homicide cases described in the book were reviewed by Domestic Homicide Review (DHR) panel members in the United Kingdom, DVDRC members in Ontario, Canada, and Fatality Review Team members in the United States. All their annual reports can be accessed online.

Readers should note that although both of these cases were domestic violence related and domestic violence is included in the title, this book is not about preventing "domestic violence." Domestic violence is broadly defined to include violence between family members, intimate partner violence (IPF), male partner violence (MPV), female partner violence, woman abuse, elder abuse, infanticide, homicide-suicide, femicide-suicide, homicide, and femicide. This book is mainly about attempts made by DVDRs to prevent femicide and femicide-suicide.

GOAL AND PURPOSES

This book has two goals. The first one is pedagogical. The second one is practical. The pedagogical goal is cognitive—motivate reflective thinking about the topics included in the book, and emotional—acknowledge feelings associated with reflective thinking about them. The practical goal of the book is to identify steps that can be taken by DVDRs toward achieving their stated purposes or intentions.

Four steps will be taken to achieve the practical goal. First, identify factors such as barriers impeding the achievement of the DVDR goal of preventing femicide. Second, identify implications for practice that will increase the fitness of DVDRs to achieve their stated objective of preventing family violence and femicide. Third, derive recommendations aimed at decreasing the probability of family violence and femicide from gendered theories aimed at explaining nonfatal and fatal partner violence against female intimate partners. Fourth, recommend policy changes that include removing impediments to the ability of DVDRs to decrease the risk of family violence and femicide.

AUDIENCE AND ORGANIZATION

This book was written with two major audiences in mind. The first is for students taking courses in criminology, social problems, injury prevention, women's studies, special topics, gender studies, and violence against women courses. The second audience is community-based practitioners to whom DVDR recommendations aimed at preventing violence against current and former female intimate partners are made.

Like most books on social science topics written by academics for an audience that includes college and university students as well as practitioners, the contents of this book are presented via chapters with subheadings, figures, tables, and a graph inserted in appropriate places in some chapters, and a more conversational style of writing that may make the book more interesting to read.

In the description of how the book is organized that follows, the contents of each chapter are briefly described, and the description ends with a link to the next chapter. As preventing femicide is one of the stated

purposes of many, if not most DVDRs, assessing their fitness for achieving this purpose requires a definition of what the book is about—its
subject matter. Specifically, it requires a definition of the major concepts
included in it. These include domestic-related homicide (murder and
manslaughter), homicide-suicide, femicide, culture, gender, ethnicity,
conflict, risk factors, and protective factors. These concepts are defined in
Chapter 1. Readers of this chapter will discover that some of the definitions are contested (e.g., homicide, homicide-suicide, femicide). Winning
these contests is important for lifesaving, political, financial, and social
scientific reasons.

For example, if advocates for women are successful in achieving public
and legislative support for naming cases in which females are murdered
as femicides, and domestic violence-related murders of females by their
male partners as male partner femicides (MPF), then criminal codes may
be changed, femicide-prevention specific funding may increase, theories
of femicide will be clearly differentiated from theories of homicide, and
the definitions of the cases reviewed by DVDR homicide case reviewers
will need to change. Also, DVDR reviewers of homicide-suicide cases can
help save lives by making recommendations aimed at preventing suicides
when the specific conditions identified in a later chapter are met.

The DVDRs defined in Chapter 1 have a history. Chapter 2 describes
the history of DVDRs in the United States, Canada, and the United
Kingdom. This chapter draws attention to the contribution made to their
establishment by media publicity on horrific murder-suicides of mothers
and children, serious gaps in the way police forces, criminal and family
courts, schools and physicians responded to these cases, the presence of
alternative ways or models of responding to them, legislation and executive orders. The absence of resistance to the establishment of DVDRs in
communities may also have been a factor influencing their establishment,
but it is not cited as such in the literature on their origin.

Frequent references to preventing femicide are made in Chapter 2.
Chapter 3 is devoted to describing theories aimed at explaining why some
males beat their female intimate partners without killing them, and others
kill female intimate partners whom they coercively control, whether they
have beaten them or not in the past.

Three theories of nonfatal male partner violence are described in the
first part of this chapter. Feminist/patriarchy theory, systems theory, and
ecological theory are presented here. When you read feminist-patriarchy
theory, expect to be reading about men who believe they are inherently superior to women and feel entitled to use violence against female partners
who resist being coercively controlled by them. Systems theory does not
really explain why men use violence against their female partners, but it
is included because it helps explain why community-based organizations

and agencies unintentionally increase the risk of male partner violence by not implementing DVDR recommendations.

Four theories of femicide are described in the second part of this chapter. The first one is an eight-stage theory in which femicides occur in the final stage when perpetrators believe they have no alternative to killing their female partners. The second one is an evolutionary psychological theory where femicide is selected by natural selection because it ensures male partner genes will be reproduced in future generations. The third one is conflict theory where (a) conflicts between intimate partners escalate to the perpetration of femicide or homicide, and (b) participation in adversarial family court proceedings that increase the intensity of mutual hostility between separating or divorcing intimate partners to the point where he kills her. The fourth one is a social ecological theory which integrates risk and protective factors included in other theories of femicide.

Femicide is a complex problem. Complex problems call for complex theories. Readers of this chapter may conclude that an ecological theory of femicide comes closest to explaining femicide because it interrelates variables or factors included in nonfatal violence and femicide theories.

Settler colonization theory is not discussed in this chapter because it is only relevant for answering the question—Why do so many indigenous men kill their female partners?—and making recommendations aimed at preventing family violence and femicide in indigenous communities where its adverse impact is greatest.

Theories are often tested by empirical research. Empirical research involves asking a question that can be answered by collecting and analyzing data quantitatively or qualitatively. Concepts such as theory, hypothesis, study design, sample selection, measurement, data analysis, findings, and conclusions are commonly used by quantitative empirical researchers. The evidence they cite is empirical. Examples of empirical research are presented in Table 4.1. Qualitative researchers often produce empirical evidence by identifying a problem worth investigating and then observing and/or interviewing nonrandomly selected samples of people contributing to, solving, or experiencing the problem. The evidence they tend to cite is qualitative. Examples of qualitative research are also presented in Chapter 4.

Chapter 4 is devoted to evaluating empirical research on preventing femicide published by two researchers who analyzed their findings qualitatively, and three others who analyzed them quantitatively. Readers of this chapter will be surprised to discover that only four out of over a thousand publications on DVDRs were empirical studies investigating their impact on femicide. Findings and other information about these four studies are presented in Table 4.1.

The information presented in Table 4.1 is accompanied by a description of its contents, including the findings. Does the description identify and describe what you learned from the table? Always check the relationship between the information conveyed by the tables included in this book with what you learn from each of them.

Table 4.1 tells two stories. One is about what is in the table. The other story is about what is not included in it. Most of the pages in this chapter are devoted to telling the first story by describing and evaluating the studies included in Table 4.1 In the final few paragraphs of the chapter, readers will be told the second story.

The second story draws attention to the fact that expertise in empirical research is not required for individuals selected to serve as members of DVDR teams, committees, and panels, and the presence of constraints upon the ability of DVDRs to achieve their stated objectives. This story ends with recommendations aimed at removing some of the constraints, creating a DVDRC composed of researchers with expertise in empirical research on family violence and femicide.

Regardless of where they are located, DVDRs operate in the shadow of a no-blame subculture where no person—with the exception of perpetrators—organization or agency is blamed for doing or not doing what they are supposed to do. Consequently, readers of this chapter should not be surprised to discover that DVDR advisory group members are not held accountable for harmful decisions they may make, and community-based organizations and agencies are not held accountable for failure to implement lifesaving recommendations.

The presence of a no-blame subculture has implications for the practice of DVDRs. Many of them are located in the offices of chief coroners or medical examiners. These DVDRs are subject to the rule of coroners. In Chapter 5, implications for the practice of reviewing homicides and making recommendations under the rule of coroners are the first of many topics investigated with practice implications in mind. Lack of accountability is one topic. Safety dilemma is another. Actually, two safety dilemmas are identified. One of them is the patient confidentiality-victim safety dilemma faced by emergency ward staff treating injuries inflicted on female patients by their male partners. The other one is the dilemma faced by victims of violence perpetrated by their current intimate partners—should they stay or leave? Risk and protective factors are implicated in femicides, and the practice implications of not collecting data on both factors are also described.

The largest number of pages is devoted to describing the practice implications of defining homicide-suicides as homicides rather than suicides. This is a long chapter because practice implications are described for many different factors. It is also an important chapter because it deals with the everyday practice of DVDR advisory group members making lifesaving recommendations to community-based organizations and agencies providing immediate protective and longer-term prevention support services to potential victims of femicide. Barriers to accessing these services are discussed in Chapter 6.

Chapter 6 describes and evaluates the thesis that barriers to accessing protective and prevention services available in the community are a potent risk factor for family violence and femicide. Evidence, cited in support of this thesis is provided by findings indicating that barriers to accessing these services are far greater in remote, northern indigenous communities than they are in southern non-indigenous communities. This is one among several factors that explain why rates of homicide and femicide in the Canadian and American indigenous communities of Alaska, the Yukon, Northwest Territories, and Nunavut are significantly higher than the femicide rates reported for non-indigenous communities in the United States and Canada.

At the same time, it is also possible that the quality of the services and resources accessed by residents in both communities may be as important as access to them. Practitioners who ask, "Is the barriers thesis also supported by findings reported by other researchers?" will find an answer to their question in this chapter.

Readers may also want to know if the recommendations made by creators of the barriers thesis to practitioners to (a) elicit disclosure of barriers experienced by their clients or patients, and (b) administer field-validated risk assessment instruments to them, are likely to result in effective management of the risk of family violence and femicide. Tentative answers to these questions are included in this chapter.

Answers to questions about barriers to resources, protective and prevention services, and the establishment of a DVDRC aimed at preventing family violence and femicide in the Nunavut First Nation are presented in Chapter 7.

Currently DVDRs created and operated by indigenous peoples are not established in any Canadian indigenous community. This chapter is devoted to providing a rationale grounded in theory and research for establishing a DVDRC in the Indigenous Arctic/Subarctic First Nation of Nunavut where violence was and is a major determinant of health. Readers of this chapter will discover the significant contribution made toward the achievement of this objective by the Royal Commission on Aboriginal Peoples (1996), the Truth and Reconciliation Commission of Canada (2016) and *Reclaiming Power and Place: The Final Report of the National Inquiry into Missing and Murdered Indigenous Women and Girls* (Government of Canada, 2019).

Chapter 7 starts with name-calling. Specifically, the names used in government publications—aboriginal and Indian—are replaced by indigenous to refer to peoples who lived in a land they called Turtle Island (North America now) long before the arrival of settler colonizers from Britain and France about 500 years ago.

The quality of life in indigenous communities before and after the arrival of settler colonizers is described in the opening pages of the chapter. Expect to learn that very high rates of one or more of the following adverse health outcomes—suicide, PTSD, incarceration, family breakdown, family violence, and femicide—are recorded for indigenous communities generally, for very remote northern Territories in Canada, and American Indian and Alaskan Native women in the United States, in particular.

Readers will also learn that settler colonizers supported by a settler colonial federal government made a major contribution toward the creation and maintenance of circumstances that resulted in the highest rates of femicide being reported for indigenous communities in Canada generally and Nunavut in particular. In addition to the use of violence and coercion by the Royal Canadian Mounted Police, readers will learn that other legal means—Numbered Treaties, the Indian Act, residential schools, and the segregation of indigenous peoples on reserves or nontraditional lands—were used to achieve the ends sought by settler colonizers.

As the adverse health effects of settler colonization were also experienced in Nunavut, readers may want to learn about how the question "What is to be done about the problem of family violence and femicide in Nunavut?" is answered in this chapter. The establishment of a DVDRC in Nunavut that requires recommendations derived in part from settler colonization theory (Figure 7.2) is an important part of the answer to this question.

Figure 7.2 is specifically designed for Nunavut. Figure 7.1 in this chapter is applicable to DVDRCs established in non-indigenous communities in the United States and Canada. A Nunavut DVDRC (Figure 2) would be the first one established in a remote indigenous community in Canada. Three of the earliest DVDRCs in the United States, Canada, and the United Kingdom are described and evaluated in Chapter 8.

The first DVDR described in Chapter 8 is the West Berkshire Domestic Homicide DHR. The second and third ones are the DVDRC in Toronto, Ontario, and the Santa Clara County Fatality Review Team (FRT) in California, respectively. Collectively, they are referred to as DVDRs. Each DVDR has an advisory group. Specifically, FRTs have teams, DHRs have panels, and DVDRCs have committees. The composition of each team, panel, and committee—who they are and how they are selected, as well as DVDR purposes, risk factors, risk management, and recommendations are reviewed.

Readers should expect to find significant similarities and differences among them. Specifically, they may want to know if any of the DVDRs made recommendations that resulted in a decrease in family violence and femicide, as well as increased information sharing between community-based organizations and agencies to whom they made recommendations.

Recommendations aimed at facilitating system change and femicide prevention are made by DVDRs located in the offices of coroners or medical examiners, attorneys general, or independently of them (e.g., DHRs). Where they are located may have implications for the practice of producing them. Only the Ontario DVDRC was located in the office of chief coroner (OCC). The practice implications of this fact are described in the closing pages of this chapter. The identification of policies aimed at preventing family violence and femicide in indigenous and non-indigenous communities is reserved for the chapter on policy.

Policies derived from Chapters 3 to 8 are described in Chapter 9. The policies described in this chapter include making DVR recommendations mandatory and creating a new emergency telephone number (988) that would require the presence of a mental health professional among police officers responding to emergency domestic violence calls. Readers are invited to think about policies that should have been included based on their reading of the preceding chapters but were not included among the ones described in this chapter.

LESSONS LEARNED

The major lesson learned in writing this introduction is that femicide is best described by the metaphor of a large rock dropped in a pond where the rock is the femicide and the ripples are the pain and suffering experienced by friends and relatives of every victim and the wider communities in which they reside.

1

+

Definitions

Several concepts are used in this book. A concept is a thought or idea that can be defined qualitatively (using words) or quantitatively (using numbers). For example, a "dangerous" male partner can be defined as being very likely to kill or inflict life-threatening injuries on his female intimate partner, or as a male partner who has used nonfatal strangulation (NFS) against his female partner resulting in her hospitalization three or more times during the past twelve months. The greater the degree of consensus on the meaning of a concept the greater its validity.

The concepts defined in this chapter are concentrated in three groups. Definitions of DVDRs and their purposes are described in the first group. Definitions in the second group refer to the violence against women that DVDRs attempt to prevent. Domestic violence-related nonfatal violence, homicide, femicide, and homicide-suicide are included in this group. Concepts included in the third group refer to factors that impact the ability of DVDRs to achieve this objective. Gender, culture, ethnicity, conflict, risk factors, and protective factors are located in this group.

DVDR GOALS AND PURPOSES

The DVDR located in the OCC of Ontario is defined as "a voluntary, diverse, multi-agency committee composed of professionals with experience and expertise in promoting the safety of family members that was created to assist the OCC in the investigation, review of deaths of persons that occur as a result of domestic violence to make non-mandatory, blame/shame free recommendations aimed at helping to prevent deaths in similar circumstances in the future."

Location-free definitions focusing on the review process itself refer to "A deliberative process for investigating the deaths of homicides and suicides caused by domestic violence; examination of systemic interventions into known incidents of domestic violence occurring in the family of the deceased prior to death; consideration of altered system responses to avert future domestic violence deaths, or for development of recommendations for facilitating coordinated, collaborative, prevention initiatives to eradicate domestic violence" (National Council of Juvenile and Family Court Judges, 1999).

In England and Wales, the DHR is defined as "A review of the circumstances in which the death of a person aged 16 or over has, or appears to have resulted from violence, abuse or neglect by (a) a person to whom he was related or with whom he was or had been in an intimate personal relationship, or (b) by a member of the same household as himself, held with a view to [preventing future homicides] by identifying and (applying) the lessons learned from [past homicides]" (Home Office, 2016 a, pp. 6–7).

An example of the domestic violence-related homicide DVDRs attempt to prevent follows:

> Adult A was a 30-year-old married woman who lived with her husband Adult B at their rented home in Reading. The couple had two children. They were described as childhood sweethearts. Adult A had a job working in a local pharmacy and Adult B worked repairing street lighting. The couple moved to their rented housing property in May 2017. Adult A had a brief history of anxiety and Adult B had a lengthy history of drug misuse, primarily cocaine. He had used the drug since the age of 19 but this was not known to his wife until very soon before she was killed. It is believed the couple had a reasonable relationship and the school and GPs who had contact with both of them reported they seemed a happy couple. However, it is believed that there were arguments between them, though there was no indication that these had ever been violent. The arguments have been described as low-level bickering but nothing out of the ordinary. In the days leading up to her murder, Adult A and Adult B had a period of sustained argument, including on the night of her murder, Adult A sent her husband a series of messages via mobile phone that related to her distrust of him and her concern about his drug use. Sometime on a night in November 2017, it is understood that the couple had an argument. At Adult B's trial, it was alleged that during the row Adult B attacked Adult A physically, punching her repeatedly and then strangling her. The injuries she received led to her death.

Domestic-intimate partner-related homicides include murder, manslaughter, and homicide-suicide. Domestic-related femicides are not defined by DVDRs. This gap is filled by the following definition: Femicide refers to murders, manslaughter, and homicide-suicides perpetrated by males against female intimate partners for any reason. The rationale for filling this gap is that preventing femicide is a major stated objective or purpose of FRTs in the United States and DVDRs in Canada. It is also a purpose of DHRs in the United Kingdom, even though it is no longer one of its explicitly stated DHR purposes in Home Office guidelines. The stated purposes described next are shared by domestic death reviews located in both types of work contexts. Their unweighted (equally important) purposes include:

- Promoting positive system change by applying lessons learned from reviewing past homicide cases in which perpetrators and/or victims contacted safety-promoting organizations and agencies, and discovering gaps or problems in collaboration, coordination and communication among organizations and agencies that were contacted by them;
- Preventing domestic violence homicides by collecting data on risk factors for lethality from police officers, and "testimonial networks" (friends, relatives, and neighbors), classifying potential victims into high and low-risk groups, and making nonbinding recommendations that safety-promoting, community-based organizations and agencies are expected but not mandated to implement;
- Increasing public awareness of femicide by publishing Annual Reports;
- Educating practitioners about precursors for lethality, and dynamics underlying domestic violence-related femicides.

In the National Domestic Violence Fatality Review online publication subtitled FAQs (Frequently Asked Questions), the "underlying objectives" of FRTs are:

- Prevent future domestic violence and domestic homicide;
- Provide safer provisions for battered women and their children;
- Hold accountable both the perpetrators of domestic violence and the multiple agencies and organizations that come into contact with the parties;
- Enhance a community's coordinated response to domestic violence and domestic homicide.

As these Big Four objectives are identified in a publication that speaks for FRTs in the United States they ought to figure prominently in any assessment that is made of them. The only question that arises at this point is why the objectives are regarded as "underlying." The opposite of underlying causes is symptoms. If underlying means that family violence and femicide have deep causal roots and that these should be addressed in FRT recommendations, then recommendations aimed at causes would be consistent with this meaning. However, if they were exclusively aimed at symptoms they would not be consistent with it.

The main objectives/purposes of DHRs identified by the United Nations Office of Drugs and Crime (UNODC, 2023, pp. 12–13) are similar to but not identical to those identified for FRTs. Specifically, the two main UNODC-identified objectives are:

- To identify lessons to be learned from the death of a person as a result of domestic violence;
- To make recommendations to improve service responses and the way that agencies from different sectors can work together to prevent domestic violence and homicide.

VIOLENCE AGAINST WOMEN

Unlike agencies such as the United Nations that attempt to prevent gender-based violence against any and all women, or agencies that attempt to prevent both domestic violence—violence between intimate partners—and family violence—violence between family members—DVDRs attempt to prevent violence against the subset of women who experience fatal and nonfatal violence perpetrated by current or former male intimate partners (husbands, cohabiters, boyfriends) with whom they may or may not reside.

Nonfatal violence is not explicitly defined, but a review of DVDR Annual Reports yields the following implicit definition: nonfatal refers to the infliction of physical violence, emotional abuse, and the use of coercive control tactics by intimate partners against each other that do not result in the death of either partner. Physical injuries varying from "minor" (a slap or push) to life-threatening and emotional and psychological injuries (e.g., stress, fear, and PTSD) are indicators of nonfatal violence, and death is an obvious indicator of fatal violence.

Fatal domestic-related violence—homicides in which the perpetrator and victim are/were intimate partners—is defined as "homicides that involve the death of a person and/or his or her child(ren) committed by the person's partners or partner from an intimate relationship" (DVDRC 2019–2020 Annual Report, p. 2).

An example of a DVDRC-defined homicide preceded by incidents of nonfatal violence is provided by the Ontario DVDRC Case # 2016-13.

"This case involved the homicide of a 21-year-old man by his 21-year-old girlfriend. The perpetrator had previously been a victim of domestic violence with another partner. There were 13 risk factors for intimate partner homicide identified."

In the 2021 Santa Clara Domestic Violence Death Review Team Report domestic violence-related deaths are broadly defined to include "all homicides: murders, murder-suicides, suicides, fatal accidents and "blue suicides" where an individual threatens to kill police officers, verbally or by the use of a weapon, and intends that the police will respond by firing upon and killing the individual making them" (p. 4).

In England and Wales, the DHR reviews "the circumstances in which the death of a person aged 16 or over has, or appears to have resulted from violence, abuse or neglect by (a) a person to whom he was related or with whom he was or had been in an intimate personal relationship, or (b) by a member of the same household as himself, held with a view to [preventing future homicides] by identifying and (applying) the lessons learned from [past homicides]" (Home Office, 2016b, pp. 6–7). This definition includes both intimate partners and family members as perpetrators and victims, but the homicide cases DHRs review usually—if not invariably—involve intimate partners as perpetrators and victims.

An example of a DHR (2018, pp. 10–13) reviewed homicide follows:

This case involves two intimate cohabiting heterosexual partners named Martin and Karen. Martin had been in contact with community health services for some time, and by the time of the murder, he had a lengthy criminal record that included 39 convictions relating to theft, damage to property, resisting arrests, breach of restraining orders, public order offences and one sexual offence against a child. Suffering from depression, he was described by the judge who sentenced him as "a jealous, controlling and violent man." Karen, his cohabiting partner, also had a criminal record, receiving cautions for offences related to theft and handling stolen goods. She had two convictions, one for criminal damage and another for wilfully insulting a justice. Her relationship with Martin was frequently interrupted by separations instigated by his abuse over a period of 11 years, and his frequent periods of imprisonment and hospitalizations for mental illness.
In September 2018, Martin phoned the police in the early hours of the morning. In that call he reported that he had mental health issues and he had "an episode and I've killed my girlfriend." Police attended Karen's home address along with paramedics and although extensive life-saving efforts were made, she was declared deceased. She had received stab wounds to her neck and chest. It is believed that she may have lost consciousness prior to being stabbed through sustained strangulation.

Homicide-suicides represent a highly gendered, ultra-rare type of homicide where 79 % of the victims are females and 15% of the cases involve multiple victims—usually children (Cotter, 2013). They are implicitly defined as homicides in DVDR Annual Reports.

An example is provided by the murder-suicide described in Case # 293 Santa Clara FRT Report:

> On November 18, 2018 the perpetrator and victim were heard arguing in the room they shared in the perpetrator's parents' home. The victim had moved to the United States from Northern Ireland after meeting the perpetrator online, to be with him, and had been in the United States for approximately one year. The perpetrator shot the victim in the head, and then shot himself in the head with a gun.

DVDR definitions of domestic violence-related homicides (murder, manslaughter, and homicide-suicide) are included in DVDR Annual Reports, but domestic-related femicides are not defined in them. This gap was filled earlier by the following definition: Femicide refers to murders, manslaughters, and homicide-suicides intentionally perpetrated by males against female intimate partners for any reason, except those perpetrated in legally defined self-defense. Femicides meeting this criterion are referred to as nonculpable femicides. The rationale for filling this gap is that preventing femicide is a major stated objective or purpose of FRTs in the United States and DVDRs in Canada. Descriptions of domestic violence-related homicide cases reviewed by the West Berkshire DHR reveal that preventing femicide is also a purpose of this DHR.

In the opening paragraph of the introduction, the metaphor of an iceberg with femicide at the tip of it was used to define femicide as an epidemic to elicit interventions aimed at ending it, such as—but not limited to—naming the intentional killings of women by men as "femicide" in criminal codes. Naming homicides by males against their female partners as femicides is important because "without a name, femicides remain hidden, impossible to speak about, count, research or develop strategies to combat it" (Radford, 2019). An example of a femicide misnamed as a homicide in the 2002 Ontario DVDRC Annual Report (Case 11) follows.

> This case of homicide involves the murder of a spouse by her husband of thirteen years. They ran a successful farming operation together with the help of other family members. However, for the past several years, the perpetrator had an unfounded belief that he would become physically disabled and as result they would lose the farm.
>
> Before the homicide he reported his concerns about depression to his physician. In response, his doctor prescribed an anti-depressant and referred him for counselling. He told a psychiatrist that he thought of suicide, and he described "catastrophic ends" to his difficulties. The perpetrator also spoke to a number of friends and neighbours about his belief that his wife was going

to leave him and take their children with her. He spoke of the fear that he would lose the farm as a result of her leaving him. He also spoke of suicide, which caused an acquaintance to refer him to a pastor for counselling.

The victim never reported any physical violence in their relationship. However, it was clear that her husband was emotionally abusive and controlling with regards to money. For some period of time leading up to the homicide, they were living separate and apart under the same roof.

On the day of the murder, the perpetrator woke the wife and asked her to help him get their van started. He walked up behind her as she exited the van and struck her on the back of her head, knocking her to the ground where she lay unconscious. He climbed on to a tractor and drove over her head. He then reversed the tractors and drove over her head again. He removed her body from the laneway with the tractor bucket and parked the tractor in the shed. He went about the remainder of the day as though nothing was amiss. Later, when a relative discovered her body, he admitted to the police upon their arrival that he killed his wife. He was subsequently arrested for first-degree murder. He pled guilty to second-degree murder in the death of his wife and was sentenced to life imprisonment.

IMPACT FACTORS

In many if not most of the DVDR reports reviewed by the author, factors other than nonfatal acts of violence, abuse, and coercive control are also implicated in the domestic-related homicide, femicide, and homicide-suicide cases reviewed by DVDR advisory group members. Definitions of these factors tend not to be included in DVDR reports. Consequently, readers are unaware of their impact on DVDR reviews of homicide and femicide cases and recommendations aimed at preventing fatal and non-fatal violence. The impact factors defined in this segment are culture, gender, ethnicity, conflict, risk factors, and protective factors.

Culture is defined as "shared, enduring meanings, language, values, norms and beliefs that characterize a society and *orients* the behavior of its members and help build and maintain their identity" (Faure & Sjostedt, 1993, p. 1; italics in original). Although it was published over 30 years ago, this definition is as valid today as it was when it was first published.

Subculture refers to values, norms, beliefs, and language that are different from those held by members of the wider society, shared by members of a variety of groups within the society, and orients different ways of behaving, life, and work styles. Examples include wine tasters, show dog owners, and mountain climbers.

Counterculture refers to values, norms, beliefs, language, and life and work styles that are opposed to (a) the values, norms, and beliefs shared by members of the wider society (e.g., street and biker gangs), and (b) the formal rules and regulation created and enforced by the bureaucrats authorized to manage formal organizations such as police forces and penitentiaries—rank-and-file police officers and penitentiary inmates, respectively.

Findings reported by Boughton (2021) led her to conclude that the subculture of DVDRs is countercultural because commitment to a "no blame/ no accountability" subculture is opposed to the blame-accountability values shared by members of the wider societal cultures of the United States, Canada, and the United Kingdom. Boughton also found "culture clash" occurs when opposing values norms and beliefs are held by representatives of organizations and agencies (e.g., criminal law enforcement and feminist treatment programs) are serving as DHR panel members (pp. 248–52).

Gender is defined as "the socially constructed roles, behaviors, expressions and identities of individuals" (Canadian Institute of Health Research, 2023). Gender identity has a significant impact on the self-concepts of individuals and couples, how they speak, act, and interact with others, the partners with whom they seek intimacy, and the discrimination they experience in their interactions with authorities and straight people. Different gender identities are held by heterosexuals, lesbians, bisexuals, gays, trans(gender), queer, Two-Spirit, and other self-gender identities. Gender is not explicitly defined in DVDR annual reports, but it is implicitly defined in a way that includes only heterosexual perpetrators and victims of domestic violence-related homicides. An example follows.

> On August 17, 2020 the male perpetrator attacked the female victim, killing her with a bat in the home they previously shared. Neighbours called 911 during the attack and emergency medical assistance arrived quickly. The victim did not survive her injuries. A week before the murder the victim had told the perpetrator to leave her home, and he had done so. The investigation revealed that two weeks prior to the murder, the perpetrator had kicked the victim in the face. The incident had not been reported to the police. The investigation also revealed that the perpetrator had prior incidents of domestic violence with the victim and other victims in prior years. The victim and perpetrator had been in a relationship for more than a year prior to separation. The perpetrator had a history of substance abuse involving methamphetamine. (Santa Clara FRT, Case 300, 2020)

Findings reported in a national Gallup Poll (2024, p. 1) indicate that about 7% of adults-including couples in intimate partner relationships identify as members of LBGTQ+ gender identity groups. As the Gallup Poll sample is a national one, it would include LBGTQ+ couples in intimate partner relationships who reside in jurisdictions served by the Santa Clara FRT.

Researchers Bender and Lauritsen (2021, p. 1) found nonfatal violence rates were two to nine times higher among self-identified LBGTQ persons, compared with heterosexuals whose gender identity was determined at birth. As nonfatal violence is a risk factor for fatal violence it is not unreasonable to expect homicide rates for intimate partners in the former group to be higher than for intimate partners in the latter group. Yet, a review of the domestic violence homicide cases reviewed by the Santa Clara, Ontario, and West Berkshire DVDRs since they appear to include cases involving self-identified LBGTQ Two-Spirit gender identity perpetrators and victims. Consequently, recommendations appropriate for preventing domestic-related homicides involving LBGTQ couples could not be made.

Ethnicity is defined as a social construct that (a) describes the shared characteristics of a group such as its culture (language, language, values, beliefs, religion, ancestry), and (b) "is located in a social hierarchy as a majority or minority group, an in-group or out group and/or a white or non-white group" (Ford & Harawan, 1993), Moreover, fatal criminal violence tends to be a more significant determinant of the health of minority, out-group, and non-white ethnic group members, than the health of white majority group member (Chapter 7 in this book).

A review of DVDR Annual Reports reveals that ethnicity is not defined in them. Moreover, the ethnicity of perpetrators and victims of domestic violence-related homicides is not revealed in the descriptions of the individual cases that are reviewed. Consequently, culturally appropriate recommendations are unlikely to be made to community-based organizations and agencies providing support and services to potential victims of homicide who are members of minority ethnic groups.

The Ontario DVDRC does not define indigenous peoples. The culturally appropriate recommendations aimed at preventing femicide against indigenous intimate female partners in Ontario appear to be grounded in unstated definitions made by police officers. In this book, indigenous peoples are defined as peoples who inhabited the United States and Canada long before they experienced colonization by white settlers. In Canada they are defined as First Nations with their distinctive cultures rather than as members of culturally diverse ethnic groups.

Conflict is a concept that is used to refer to mutually hostile feelings among two or more individuals, groups and nations have for each other. Conflict should not be confused with conflict resolution or settlement. They are separate concepts. In the present context, conflict resolution refers to agreements reached by the use of peaceful means, such as discussion, negotiation, or mediation that yield stable, long-lasting peace between intimate partners. Settlement refers to agreements reached by the threat or use of violence, and/or the use or coercive control tactics that result in unstable ceasefires. Some conflicts between intimate partners are functional by changing the conditions or circumstances that caused them. Others are dysfunctional because they yield outcomes that harm one or both partners. For some people, conflict is functional when it results in separation or divorce. For others, separation or divorce is dysfunctional (Ellis & Anderson, 2005, pp. 1–11).

Protective factors are defined as individual, relationship, and community-level factors that decrease the probability and risk of femicide. Individual protective factors for femicide include men who believe in and value gender equality. Relationship factors include the marital status (married, separated, divorced) of couples. In DVDR Annual Reports, risk factors are implicitly defined as factors that increase the risk or odds of femicide. Separation initiated by female partners and nonfatal violence used against them by their male partners is identified as significant, noncausal risk factors in many if not most DVDR Annual Reports. Noncausal risk factors for femicides perpetrated earlier are used to predict and prevent future femicides. Some of the risk factors for earlier and later femicides can be treated or modified by appropriate interventions (e.g., alcohol abuse, depression), while others are not modifiable (e.g., skin color).

Readers should also note that the risk factors identified in DVDR Annual Reports refer to "incidents" rather than "patterns" of nonfatal violence and coercive control when most contemporary domestic violence theorists and researchers would probably support the hypothesis that knowledge of patterns is a more reliable predictor of femicide than knowledge of incidents. Community-based protective factors include access to community-based housing, employment, and daycare resources enabling mothers to live safer and comparatively better lives living separate and apart from violent male partners. Protective factors are not defined in DVDR Annual Reports. Consequently, risk assessments based on the presence and potency of risk and protective factors are rarely if ever included in them.

LESSONS LEARNED

Readers of this chapter will have learned two lessons. One, apart from domestic-related homicides, DVDR Annual Reports are unlikely to help them understand exactly what all the other concepts included in this chapter mean because they were not explicitly defined. Two, DVDRs are attempting to decrease femicides by defining them as homicides.

2

✝

History

Following the creation of death reviews involving children as victims, the first domestic violence FRT in the United States was created in 1994 in Santa Clara County, California. In 2021, 200 or more FRTs were operating in 43 states in the United States (McHardy & Hofford, 1999) The first DVDRC was created in 2003 in the province of Ontario, Canada. They are now present in six of the ten provinces in Canada. In the United Kingdom, DHRs were legally created in 2011. There are now over 141 DHRs in England and Wales.

A perusal of the literature on FRTs in the United States, DVDRCs in Canada, and DHRs in the United Kingdom (England and Wales) reveals their origins can be traced to the presence of many factors that vary in their salience.

A short list of the most highly weighted—most important—factors is likely to include media publicity and pressure; family and feminist campaigning aimed at preventing future high-profile femicide suicides; system gaps in the delivery of services and support to victims of intimate partner violence; presence of alterative models of investigating and responding to patterns of coercively controlling, physically injurious and psychologically abusive male partner conduct; and a new cultural change paradigm published by advocates for DVDRs. A description of each of these factors follows in the order in which they were identified.

MEDIA PUBLICITY

Shocking and alarming media publicity of multiple homicide-suicides involving mothers and children as victims of separating or separated fathers was a precursor for legislation, executive orders, and a "Consultation-DHR Guidance Document" (Home Office, 2006a) creating DHRs.

The specific high-profile cases widely publicized by the media included the 1990 Charan case in San Francisco (Websdale et al., 1999), the 2003 Pemberton Review (Walker et al., 2008) in West Berkshire, and the 1996 May-Iles case in Ontario, Canada (Sampson, 2003).

On January 15, 1990, Joseph Charan killed his wife Veena who he physically assaulted on an ongoing basis, and then committed suicide in front of the Excelsior elementary school in which his daughter was a student. For about 15 months before her death, Veena sought help from a variety of community-based organizations and agencies, including the police. Shortly before he killed her, Charan was convicted of felony assault; put on probation; received a restraining order; spent four days in jail; violated court orders; and attempted to kidnap his child from school.

In September 2002, Julia Pemberton separated from her husband Alan. She was separating from him because of the physical violence, coercive control, and psychological abuse he used against her for some time. Her husband Alan strongly opposed the separation. Following their separation, he threatened to kill her several times verbally by telephone, as well as in writing threats on one of the affidavits she submitted for an injunction. He also glued the locks on her family home. On July 7, 2003, Julia applied for the renewal of a non-molestation order, but on the basis of Alan's undertaking to the court, he was given permission to park on the driveway in order to pick up his son William for a driving lesson.

Julia repeatedly reported Alan's criminal conduct to the Thames River Police who did not charge Alan with any offence. Nor did they interview him about her safety concerns or communicate her fears to the Police Domestic Violence Coordinator. Julia also communicated her concerns about her safety to her general practitioner, and the school her son William attended. Neither reported her concerns to the police or social services.

On November 18, 2003, Alan arrived at the family home where Julia and her son lived and parked on the driveway. Julia saw he had a gun and heard shots. She made a 999 call to the police. Unarmed officers arrived 40 minutes later to find William's dead body on the driveway. Prior to the arrival of the police, Alan shot the doors of the house open, entered the home, shot Julia, and then himself to death. Armed police officers entered the house the next day—six hours after Julia made the 999 call—to find Alan and Julia dead inside.

In addition to nationwide media publicity, campaigns started by Julia's family and friends resulted in the creation of a DHR by the West Berkshire Safety Communities Partnership. In 2008, the partnership published a report. The report was also reviewed by Walker et al. (2008). They found serious gaps in the police response to multiple reports of death threats and violence made to them by Julia and a lack of communication and coordination between different ranks of police officers, police officers, and the domestic violence coordinator attached to the police force, and among medical practitioners, the school William attended, and social services.

Arlene May, a 38-year-old mother of five children, was involved in a two-year relationship with Randy Iles. During their relationship, Arlene experienced a pattern of physical violence, psychological abuse, and coercive control. On November 14, 1995, Arlene was assaulted by Iles, and for the first time, she reported the assault to the police. Three months later, Randy Iles shot her to death. During the last three months of her life Arlene attempted to protect herself and her children by initiating proceedings in criminal court that resulted in Randy's appearance in court 11 times. Despite the threat he posed, he was granted bail on four occasions—with surety being set at 200 pounds sterling on his last bail hearing—the one he was on when he killed Arlene (Sampson, 2003, p. 78).

SYSTEM GAPS

In the Charan case, the first of four "essential gaps" and a review of "case files and public testimony," revealed a lack of communication and coordination among "multiple agencies and organizations including the police, criminal and family courts, probation and social services" (Websdale et al., 1999, p. 63).

In the Pemberton case, Walker et al. (2008) found serious gaps in the police response to multiple reports of death threats and violence made to them by Julia, and a lack of communication and coordination among the police, domestic violence coordinator attached to the police force, medical practitioners, the school, and social services. The system gaps referred to in the FRT and DHR were also reported by the creators of the Ontario DVDRC.

ALTERNATIVE MODELS

To creators of contemporary DVDRs, widely publicized media articles, reports, and editorials about these cases, as well as the investigations that followed them, indicated that they must do something different from what was being done to prevent femicides by the criminal and civil (family) justice systems, as well as community-based organizations and agencies that responded to them. Doing something different required "A paradigm shift from a culture of blame to a culture of safety in which domestic violence deaths are viewed through the lens of preventive accountability" (Websdale et al., 1999, p. 61).

Blame-free postmortem investigations being conducted by investigators of airplane crashes and coroners or medical examiners in the United States and Canada, as well as "lessons learned" by them aimed at "preventing deaths in similar circumstances" in the future, served as models of investigation deemed worthy of emulation by multi-agency DVDRs in these countries (Dawson, 2003; Websdale et al., 1999).

The paradigm shift referred to earlier, required a coordinated, collaborative community response to domestic violence generally, and femicide in particular. An existing model of such a response was provided by The Duluth Coordinated Community Response (CCR) (Pence & Paymar, 1993).

LEGISLATION

Many DVDRs are created by enabling legislation. In the United Kingdom, DHRs were introduced by section 9 of the Domestic Violence, Crime and Victims Act 2004. The latest iteration of statutory guidance governing the process of DHR reviews is provided by the Home Office (2016). Following a homicide that meets the criteria for a DHR review, a DHR can be commissioned by Community Safety Partnerships located in over 200 jurisdictions (cities, regions, counties) in England and Wales.

Santa Clara County was the first county to establish an FRT in 1994 following a request made by the United States, Department of Justice to the Santa Clara Domestic Violence Council to establish an FRT in this county. In the United States many FRTs are created by enabling legislation. For example, the Washington, D.C., FRT was created by DC Law 14-296 (Uniform Interstate Enforcement of Domestic Violence Protection Orders Act of 2002). The source of homicide cases reviewed by this FRT is the Office of the Chief Medical Examiner. The Code of Virginia, Title 32.1 permits the establishment of an FRT "upon the initiative of "any local or regional law-enforcement agency, department of social services, emergency medical service agency, attorney for the Commonwealth's office, community services board or official with the Adult Protective Services." The source of homicides reviewed by the FRT includes deaths investigated by the Office of the Chief Medical Officer.

California's amended Penal Code, sections 11163.3 9a and 1163.5 mandates the creation of domestic homicide and homicide-suicide fatality review teams in all 58 counties and provides for the coordination of community-based organizations and for the purpose of preventing these fatal outcomes.

In Canada, the Ontario DVDRC was created following recommendations made by juries at two major inquests resulting in the deaths of multiple victims of domestic violence-related homicides, and the Report of the Joint Committee on Domestic Violence "to review and advise the Office of the Chief Coroner of Ontario on all domestic violence fatalities that occur in Ontario" (Ontario DVDRC Annual Report, 2002, p. 4). The OCC of Ontario is the sole source of the homicide cases reviewed by the Ontario DVDRC. This DVDRC is part of the OCC of Ontario to whom it reports. The chief coroner reports to the solicitor general of Ontario.

Jaffee et al. (2008, p. 5) identify eight different pathways to the creation of domestic homicide reviews, including a legislative mandate, a domestic violence service provider, grant funding, and an administrative order of the court. Legislative mandate seems to be the most frequently used pathway to the creation of DVDRs in statewide and large city jurisdictions. In counties, small cities, and rural areas DVDRs are created by domestic violence agencies and organizations and concerned members of the community funded by private and public grants" (Pow et al., 2015, p. 5).

Twenty-five years after they were established by these means, FRTs emphasizing noncriminal justice system interventions were active in all but four of the states in the United States (Websdale et al., 2019). However, in 2005 some of the same historical factors were involved in the establishment of the multidisciplinary, coordinated community response, perpetrator-focused High Risk Response Team femicide prevention model that prioritized criminal justice system interventions. For example, factors involved in the establishment of the Newburyport, Massachusetts, High-Risk Team included media reports on the murder of Dorothy Giunta-Cotter by her estranged husband and his subsequent suicide, plus the belief that the existing programs (including FRTs) were ineffective in preventing femicides of women "who did everything right to protect themselves" (Rosenfeld, 2022). A modified version of the high-risk team model is included in the federally funded (Department of Justice, Office of Violence Against Women) Domestic Violence Prevention Demonstration Initiative, but a modified version of an FRT model is not.

The change "blowing in the wind" is in the direction of federal funding of programs prioritizing the criminal justice system response to preventing femicide such as the high-risk team model, and any other model where police officers use the Lethality Assessment Screen or the Danger

Assessment 2 to locate perpetrators in risk categories. Such programs may include the use of preventive detention (jailed before being convicted of a crime), GPS monitoring of perpetrators, and dangerousness hearings based on LAS or Danger Assessment 2 risk categories aimed at preventing contact between high-risk perpetrators and victims.

Finally, it is relevant to note that DVDRs were established as an alternative to exclusive reliance on the criminal justice system response to family violence and femicide. The source of the alternative prevention model selected for implementation was based on the National Transportation Safety Board's response to airplane crashes. A model grounded in "the community's much longer experience" with a public health response to interpersonal violence was either not considered or considered and rejected by creators of FRTs in the United States. In this model, family violence would be framed as a "pervasive public health challenge [that] exposes individuals to a broad range of physical, emotional and cognitive health problems [as well as] the transmission and progression of infectious diseases such as STIs and HIV/AIDS," and whose effects reverberate through families, communities and nations and across generations" Mercy et al., 2017, p. 5).

A life-course model of violence prevention could also have been reviewed with a view to its implementation. An example of a life-course model (Niolan et al., 2017) is provided by the response to preventing and the loss of life, damage to property and the environment caused by hurricanes. Just as the hurricane model requires the collection of data on the birth, life, and death of hurricanes, a life-course model requires the collection of data on the life course of victims of femicide.

LESSONS LEARNED

One important lesson learned is that communities can come together and work collaboratively in their attempts to solve social problems in their communities. More generally, it is important to learn about and remember the history of DVDRs because it may help us avoid repeating history by making agents of the criminal justice system mainly, if not exclusively responsible for femicide. This lesson can be traced to philosopher George Santanya who learned that "those who cannot remember the past are bound to repeat it."

3

+

Theory

Declaration: This review is being conducted by an academic whose publications on male partner violence (MPV) against women suggest he favors feminist ecological theories of femicide that include conflict as a relationship factor.

The relevance of theory for preventing family violence and femicide was succinctly stated by the United Nations Office on Drugs and Crime (UNODC; 2023, p. 41) in the following modified terms: poor understanding of the dynamics of gender-based violence against women (GBVAW) results in DVDR recommendations inadequate to prevent or decrease the probability and risk of male violence against their female intimate partners. The UNODC statement refers to nonfatal GBVAW by male intimate partners. In this chapter, explanatory theories of nonfatal MPV and femicide are presented under the subheadings of male partner violence, femicide, and femicide-suicide. The three theories are reviewed for the purpose of informing DVDR recommendations aimed at prevention. Systems theory is included with feminist/patriarchy and evolutionary theories of MPV under this subheading because it helps explain the near absence of collaborative and coordinated responses of community-based organizations and agencies to DVDR recommendations.

MALE PARTNER VIOLENCE

Theories of MPV are presented first because many empirical researchers and DVDR investigators report findings indicating that MPV is a potent predictor of femicide. For example, researchers Graham et al. (2022) cite findings indicating that "two to three-quarters of female victims of homicide were abused by the perpetrator prior to being killed" (p. 409).

When MPV is perpetrated, it invariably precedes femicide in time. This seems like a good reason for presenting theories of MPV first.

Patriarchy

Grounded partly in historical evidence, the theory of "the patriarchy" created by Dobash and Dobash (1979, p. 46) is a dual-focus theory in the sense that it focuses on husbands as perpetrators and community reactions to violence against women that help maintain an approximation to the medieval patriarchal family. The medieval family household was one in which husbands were heads of households, and husbands who used violence against wives who disobeyed them were immune to punishments by agents of the state so long as the violence did not result in serious injury.

Empirical evidence of approximation to the medieval patriarchal family in the 1970s was provided by findings from interviews with a non-random sample of one hundred and nine residents of shelters for abused women who sought help from a variety of community-based organizations and agencies.

Dobash and Dobash (1979, p. 43) define "the patriarchy" as a set of interrelated, differentiated, hierarchically organized legal, business, political, and educational institutions in which women are located at the bottom of the hierarchy in all of them. The cultural values, norms, and beliefs legitimating this arrangement maintain the subordination of women generally, and of intimate female partners in particular. In the institution of the family, "physical violence is one of the most brutal and explicit expressions of patriarchal domination" (p. ix).

Dobash and Dobash (1979, pp. 162–42) reported findings indicating that the presence of patriarchy today is revealed by responses to MPV by police officers who are reluctant to police relationships in which partners end up killing their female partners; by healthcare professionals who simply blame individual men and not the wider patriarchal society for using physical (criminal) violence against female partners; and by social workers, counselors, relatives, and friends committed to maintaining a family form in which female partners are coercively controlled and abused physically and psychologically by their male partners.

Principles adopted by the organizations and agencies vary. Only the principles adopted by advocates for women, and shelters for abused women include the principle, "To encourage women to determine their own futures and help women achieve them" (Dobash & Dobash, 1979,

p. 124). Dobash and Dobash's (1979) recommendations derived from the patriarchy would be limited to community-based organizations and agencies adopting this principle of liberation.

In a book published 11 years after the publication of *Violence Against Women*, Sylvia Walby (1990, p. 20) defined patriarchy as "a system of social arrangements and practices in which men dominate, oppress and exploit women."

For feminist researcher Walby (1990), patriarchy is characterized by the presence of six interrelated arrangements. The state with its "systematic bias towards patriarchal interests in its policies and actions" is one of them. Male partner violence experienced by women is "systematically condoned and legitimated by the state's refusal to intervene against it," is another arrangement. Taken together, the patriarchal arrangements she describes explain both gender inequality in which females are subordinate to their male intimate partners, and the killing of female partners who challenge their subordination by seeking liberation through separation and divorce (p. 1).

Although it was published many years ago, the Dobash and Dobash theory of "the patriarchy," is at the heart of contemporary radical feminist explanations of violence against women (Carter, 2014; Corrado et al., 2016; DeKeseredy et al., 2017; Gavigan, 2013; Hunnicutt, 2009; National Resource Center on Domestic Violence, 2021; Taylor & Jasinski, 2011).

According to Heise (1998), gender inequality and misogyny remain the main motives for femicide, and the "context and circumstances of intimate partner femicide" reflect these motives. Feminist researchers Long et al. (2017, p. 16) go so far as to state that DVDR recommendations aimed at preventing future femicides derived solely from investigations of the context and circumstances present in past femicides are unlikely to be effective if the precondition of disrupting gender inequality is not met.

The positive contribution made to promoting the safety of women by facilitating communication, collaboration, and coordinating interventions by shelters for abused women, healthcare providers, and other family violence prevention agencies and organizations, was not included in the patriarchy theories described here. These factors are central to the systems theory described in the segment that follows.

Systems

In this book systems theory is used to explain why it is difficult for DV-DRs to promote "system change" in the direction of preventing MPV and femicide by making recommendations to formal and informal organizations and agencies whose goals include the achievement of these objectives. A collectivity or group of organizations and agencies who provide family violence prevention services constitute a social system in the sense that their responses to MPV and femicide influence—and are influenced by—the responses made by other organizations and agencies with the same objectives in the same jurisdiction.

Social systems theory is applied in a context in which victims and perpetrators with multiple problems associated with MPV and femicide contact or become involved with some organizations and agencies providing the same type of intervention (e.g., mental healthcare), and others providing different interventions (e.g., law enforcement and women's advocacy programs, subsidized housing). In West Berkshire, the number of organizations, agencies, professionals, and practitioners varied between twelve (2018 Report) and three (2008 Report). In the Ontario 2018 DVDRC Report the number varies between eight and two. The average number of involvements in both cases was four.

The Santa Clara FRT Reports do not include information on victims and perpetrator contacts with community-based organizations and agencies. However, the composition of death review team members suggests that victims and perpetrators could have contacted one or more of 45 organizations and agencies, including five different police departments and community-based family violence prevention agencies. The specific police department contacted before the homicide case was reviewed was not named.

A proposition derived from systems theory states that the greater the number of organizations, agencies, professionals, and practitioners contacted by victims and perpetrators, the more difficult it will be for FRTs, DVDRs, and DHRs to facilitate system change.

Systems theory also draws attention to the prioritizing of confidentiality over safety as a factor impeding information exchange between community-based organizations and agencies providing support and services to victims and perpetrators. The sources of this imbalance include legislation and confidentiality rules adopted by community-based organizations and agencies providing support and services to victims and perpetrators of MPV and femicide. For example, staff in women's shelters are reluctant to provide information to staff in other agencies because shelter residents are assured that the information communicated to shelter staff is confidential. Patient confidentiality may also help explain why emergency ward staff in hospital staff are reluctant to share information on patients they treated for injuries inflicted by male partners who murdered them sometime afterward (Pobutsky et al., 2014, p. 79).

Many barriers prevent or minimize disclosure by physicians generally, and physicians staffing emergency wards in particular. Barriers include privacy legislation requiring the permission of a patient-victim to consent to the disclosure of health-related information; ethical and legal obligations by the code and ethics of professionalism by medical associations, and advice of the medical protective associations who advise physicians not to "disclose patient information to the police or other third party unless there is patient consent or disclosure is legally required." Additionally, civil and criminal legislation may impede information sharing on victims and/or perpetrators (e.g., Victim's Bill of Rights, California, Freedom of Information. And Protection of Privacy Act, Ontario; Canadian Medical Protective Association, 2023).

One or more of these barriers may be the reason for the finding that only one-third (n=45) of the homicide cases reviewed by the Hawaii FRT "had documentation of prior violence from medical reports" (Pobutsky et al., 2014, p. 79).

Support for concluding that information relating to risk management is least likely to be shared by healthcare professionals and practitioners, police services and social services is provided by the results of the Home Office (2016, pp. 25, 26) survey of a sample of 190 DHRs who identified them as "having communication and information sharing issues both intra (within) and inter (between) agencies." Social system theory identifies the absence or lack of information sharing as a major barrier to coordinating multi-agency interventions aimed at preventing family violence and femicide.

Finally, systems theory draws the attention of DVDRs to factors beyond their control that create barriers to information exchange between community-based organizations and agencies to whom they make recommendations. These barriers are most likely to be created in communities experiencing (a) decreases in funding for family violence prevention organizations and agencies (b) increases in the demand for services provided by them, and (c) the replacement of "flexible funding to meet designated needs by short-term contracts." Taken together, these three factors "increase competition for government funding among community based voluntary organizations and agencies" (Elson & Carmichael, 2022, p. 20). Increased competition tends to impede information sharing.

Findings reported by systems theory researchers Elson and Carmichael (2022) indicate that "short-term, competitive, outcome-driven contracts" applied for by many, but granted only to the successful few are unlikely to be one in which information between organizations and agencies flows freely (Elson & Carmichael, 2022).

To this point, two of the questions identified in the introduction have been answered by patriarchy theory and systems theory. A review of the literature on IPF reveals that a more complex theory is required for two reasons. One, patriarchy theory cannot explain why the vast majority of men do not murder their female intimate partners (Brittney, 2018, p. 13), and national (US) victimization surveys reveal that over 80% of women sampled do not report experiencing male partner criminal violence (Tjaden & Thoennes, 2000). Two, systems theory cannot explain why male partners residing in the same community include many who do not kill or use criminal violence against their female partners and some who do (Brittney, 2018, p. 13).

Findings based on a review of the contemporary literature on IPF by Bandelli (2017) and Corrado et al. (2016) led them to conclude that a more complex theory of femicide is required to answer these questions. The complex theory that includes characteristics of perpetrators and victims, their relational history, and sociocultural environment are included in ecological theories of femicide.

Ecological

The ecological model for preventing femicide published by Dawson (2016) states the risk of femicide varies with interactions among individual, relationship, community, and society levels. The complexity of femicide is addressed by this theory (p. 2). However, Dawson (2016) does not derive recommendations aimed at addressing the root causes of IPF, such as "rectifying structural inequalities, gender stereotypes and discrimination against women and girls" (p. 2) that are located at the societal level. Instead, DVDR recommendations are limited to "identifying potential improvements in systems" (p. 2).

The ecological model created by Heise (2011) includes levels for male and female partners as individuals, the relationship between them, macro (societal) and community levels. Patriarchy theory would be included at the societal level, and systems theory at the community level. This ecological theory requires DVDRs to make recommendations appropriate to each of these levels, including recommendations aimed at males and females as individuals, and as intimate partners. It also improves upon earlier ecological models (Dawson, 2016; Stout, 1992) in at least three ways.

First, it makes a two-stage process of intervention possible. In this process, DVDR recommendations aimed at preventing violence against the victim would include a caveat that calls to the police for protection may result in subsequent beatings by perpetrators—and recommendations aimed at preventing the use of violence by perpetrators would also include a caveat about the effects of police interventions upon the victim, his arrest, being charged and denied bail may result in a loss of needed family income (Eckhardt et al., 2013).

Second, locating conflict in the relationship level requires DVDR recommendations that focus on the couple (Bartholomew et al., 2009; Goode, 1971, p. 632).

Third, conflict and attempts to settle them are endemic in all social relationships, including relationships between intimate couples (Avtgis

& Rancer, 2010; Ellis & Anderson, 2005; Straus, 1979). Arguments are frequently used to settle interpersonal conflicts (Alfano, 2006; Beaupre, 2014; Brittney, 2018; Johnson & Hotton, 2003; Nicolaidis et al., 2003; Violence Policy Center, 2021), but very few arguments are settled by murder, manslaughter, and homicide-suicide (Campbell et al., 2007; Ellis, Stuckless, & Smith, 2015). The inclusion of "conflict and conflict excalation" might well increase the contribution made toward preventing precursors of femicide such as nonfatal MPV.

Heise's (2011) ecological theory also invites domestic violence death reviews to consider making recommendations aimed at promoting the safety of victims of MPV who do not want to separate from their physically abusive and coercive controlling male partners. Contemporary explanations of "Why does she stay?" include love as a valid answer to this question (Kuennen, 2013; Towns & Adams, 2000). Moreover, a majority of mothers want to stay with the partner they love but also want the violence to stop (Bruton & Tyson, 2017; Campbell et al., 1998; Cavanagh, 2003; Goodmark, 2007)

In sum, ecological theories of femicide address its complexity and serve as a rationale for domestic violence death review recommendations aimed at (a) changing the behavior of perpetrators who instigate arguments resulting in femicide; (b) changing the behavior of victims by persuading them not to communicate the decision to separate while they are involved in perpetrator instigated, face-to-face arguments over his possessiveness and coercive controlling behavior; (c) couple participation in programs that teach couples how to argue, and "still behave decently towards each other" (Ellis et al., 2015, pp. 144–45); and (d) promoting the safety of victims who experienced MPV but who want to keep living with partners who use violence against them. The perpetrators discussed in the segment that follows kill their female intimate partners. Theories aimed at answering the question "Why?" are also discussed.

FEMICIDE

Eight Stage

The eight-stage theory was created by Moncton-Smith (2021). Her inductive theory is derived from a sample of 372 male partner-perpetrated homicide cases reviewed "in the media, homicide reviews and risk factors identified by police officers administering DASH (risk assessment instrument) to victims." These data, plus "recurring themes revealed by analysis," produced eight sequenced stages describing a move in the direction of the end stage of IPF perpetration.

The stages are named and indicators are described in brackets for each of the eight stages: pre-relationship (history of coercive controlling behavior, abuse, or stalking present); early relationship (normal romantic expectations and activities); relationship (commitment of partners to each other legitimating the right of the male partner to control the female partner); trigger event (withdrawal of commitment via actual, imagined or threatened separation by the female partner that challenges male partner control); escalation (attempt to regain control by increasing the frequency and severity of abuse, control and/or stalking); change in thinking (reacts to the perceived irretrievable loss of control entailed by separation or divorce by stalking that elicits "last chance thinking" where killing her is perceived to be the only alternative available to him); planning (taking concrete steps to create opportunities for killing her and obtaining the means used to achieve this end); homicide (may involve extreme levels of violence even by historically nonviolent male partners).

Progression to the end stage of homicide is not inevitable because even after reaching the stage of "last chance thinking," changing opportunities and circumstances may decrease the intensity of the male partner's motivation to kill his female partner. Consequently, DVDRs can make recommendations appropriate for the stage reached in the progression toward homicide. Moreover, although the risk of separation-related homicide increases significantly as male partners progress through the sequence of stages, there is time—about four months—for DVDRs to make recommendations aimed at ending the progression before it reaches the stage of "last chance thinking."

The inductive eight-stage theory created by Moncton-Smith (2020) is clearly the product of creative thinking. At the same time, some readers may have detected a few problems with it. First, the findings she reports are based partly on risk factors reported by police officers administering DASH to female victims of MPV. Evidence cited in this book indicates that this risk assessment instrument does no better than chance—tossing a coin—in predicting femicide.

Second, the theory would be more persuasive if it was also supported by information provided by interviews with perpetrators of femicides and survivors of attempted femicides.

Third, as cutoff points for each stage are not defined or even suggested, the validity of Moncton-Smith's stage theory is compromised when indicators of earlier stages are present in later stages and vice versa. Fourth, planned femicides are rarely described in DVDR Annual Reports, but the eight-stage theory can explain only planned femicides. Five, data on relationships (Stages 1 to 3) requires the collection of data from both—not just one—intimate partner. Finally, a pattern of male partner coercive control is conceived of as the major explanatory factor for intimate partner femicides, but its source or origin is not identified. This gap is filled by the evolutionary psychological theory.

Evolutionary Psychological

In societies all over the world women who initiate separations from their male intimate partners or are believed by them to be sexually involved with other men, are killed more frequently than women who reside with them, and are sexually monogamous. In other words, globally, the context (intimate relationship) and motives (jealousy and possessiveness) for femicide are the same (Daly & Wilson, 1988, pp. 202–204). "Psychological theorizing informed by modern evolutionary theory" is used by Daly and Wilson to explain the biological origins of these motives in the context of intimate relationships where, for men, paternity is uncertain. Specifically, natural selection maximizes the reproductive fitness of men who ensure that only their genes are reproduced by the children of the women with whom they are involved in intimate relationships.

To this end, natural selection selected the male-specific mindset of male sexual proprietariness (MSP). MSP is defined as "an encompassing mindset . . . and a pervasive attitude toward intimate relationships in which intimate female partners are thought of as property men are entitled to own, in the same way that slave owners were entitled to own slaves" (Wilson & Daly, 1992, p. 302). Male sexual jealousy is a means of solving the paternity-uncertainty problem by preventing female partner infidelity and desertion. Consequently, it serves the evolutionary end of reproductive success.

The dynamic involved is described in these terms: Sexual jealousy is aroused when female intimate partners violate biologically determined MSP rights. Male partners attempt to ensure paternity certainty by punishing female partners who violate them. Femicide is the most extreme form of punishment perpetrated on female partners who violate MSP rights.

The inclusion of femicide among the punishments administered by male partners is "paradoxical" because it simultaneously serves and doesn't serve the evolutionary end of inclusive fitness. As a manifestation of MSP motivated by jealousy—"If I can't have you, no one can" (Wilson & Daly, 1992, p. 86)—femicide serves the end of inclusive fitness ability of a person to transmit genes to the next generation (Hamilton, 1964) of an evolved psychological mechanism (such as MSP). However, as an evolved psychological mechanism (such as MSP) that "overstepped the bounds of utility," femicide may serve the end of demonstrating male domination but not the end of inclusive fitness (Daly & Wilson, 1988, pp. 12–13; Ellis et al., 2015, pp. 64–65).

At this point a reader may conclude that Daly and Wilson (1988) are saying that the evolved psychological mechanism of MSP is the only factor responsible for fatal/ nonfatal violence MPV and control of female intimate partners in all societies, including the three societies in which DV-DRs are being reviewed in this book. However, Daly and Wilson (1988) also state that natural selection created a human mind capable of taking the social circumstances or contexts into account prior to behaving. Consequently, MSP-related femicides are more likely to be perpetrated in communities where the social, economic and reputational costs of perpetration are perceived as being higher and more certain to be experienced than the rewards of perpetration (Daly & Wilson, 1988, pp. 230–31, 250–51). Inclusive fitness is maximized for male partners who are members of societies and communities where "the tolerance for male partner violence is low and the social and personal costs are high" (Johnson, 2012, p. 335). The mechanisms involved are deterrence and self-control.

In sum, both biological and sociological (contextual social and structural) factors are integrated in the Daly and Wilson (1988) evolutionary psychological theory of femicide (Johnson, 2012).

A review of this theory elicits two responses. First, their evolutionary psychological theory is limited to explaining femicides involving female intimate partners of child-bearing age as victims. DVDR recommendations, on the other hand, are aimed at preventing femicide perpetrated against intimate female partners of any age.

Second, the theory is designed to explain "social conflict homicides" (Daly et al., 1982, p. 11). Conflict is a relational concept. In the present context, the conflict is between sexually jealous male partners who attempt to achieve "paternity confidence" by possessing and controlling the sexual behavior of female partners, and who become enraged to the point of killing those who threaten paternity certainty by their infidelity on the one hand, and on the other hand, female partners who end their male partner's quest for paternity certainty by infidelity and desertion. Female intimate partners also experience sexual jealousy, but differently. Specifically, they are jealous of the time, money, and attention devoted to other women, but not so much about their sexual infidelity. Nothing in the mindset inculcated in women by natural selection motivates them to resist male partner attempts to possess and control them, or to seek liberation from entrapment by coercively controlling male partners. So, where is the conflict in conflict femicides?

The answer to this question is presented in a chapter included in a book edited by Radford and Russell titled *Femicide: The Politics of Woman Killing* (Wilson & Daly, 1992), which was published a few years after Daly and Wilson published their book on homicide in 1988.

Conflict

In a chapter titled "Till Death Do Us Part," Wilson and Daly (1992) described what has come to be known as a "slip-up theory of femicide" (Graham et al., 2022, p. 418). In this theory, femicide is described as "just the tip of the iceberg where for every murdered wife, hundreds are beaten, coerced and intimidated by male intimate partners." The Wilson and Daly (1992) slip-up theory states "Men strive to control women. . . . Women struggle to resist coercion and maintain their choices, there is brinkmanship and risk of disaster in any such [conflict], and homicides by spouses of either sex may be considered the slips in this dangerous game." In this theory, femicides are regarded as "relatively rare and extreme manifestations of the same basic conflicts [involving adultery, jealousy and male proprietariness] that inspire sub-lethal [male partner] violence on a much larger scale."

As most social scientists would agree that conflict is endemic or normal in human social relationships (Ellis & Anderson, 2005), and findings indicating that arguments over these issues are a potent trigger for femicides (Nicolaidis et al., 2003), the slip-up theory of conflict would appear to be worthy of inclusion in an integrated theory of femicide.

Supporters of the slip-up theory can facilitate its inclusion by responding to the following four concerns. One, reference to "homicides of spouses of either sex," gives the impression that male and female partners are equally likely to kill each other, but findings reported by the US Bureau of Justice Statistics (2022, p. 1) indicate that female intimate partners were 5 times more likely to be murdered by an intimate partner than males. Statistic Canada (2023, p. 9) researchers found that 79% of the victims of intimate partner homicide occurring between 2009 and 2022 (n=1,223 victims) were female and 21% were male. As slip-ups that result in death are made mainly by female intimate partners, the gender-neutral statement referred to earlier should be replaced by one that reflects the gendered findings reported here.

Two, mechanisms responsible for the escalation of nonfatal violence to femicide are not identified. They are identified by Bosch (2017) and Winstock and Eisikovits (2008) and could be included in the Wilson and Daly (1992) theory.

Three, state that the theory is not designed to explain femicides that are planned.

Four, resolve the contradiction between evolutionary psychological theory which states that femicide was "naturally selected because of its benefits for reproduction," and the slip-up theory which states that femicide occurs as a slip or mistake during the use of nonfatal violence by both intimate partners (Graham et al., 2022, p. 418). Perhaps, coercive control motivated by sexual jealousy is resisted by female partners. Resistance results in conflicts involving the mutual use of violence where femicides occur as a result of slip-ups. DVDR recommendations derived from social conflict theory should focus on peaceful conflict resolution, and those derived from evolutionary psychological theory should focus on increasing community intolerance for MPV generally, and particularly against mothers who decide to end their relationship with violence and coercively controlling partners.

For mothers with dependent children, the end of a relationship via separation and divorce often means participation in separation and divorce proceedings that can increase the probability and risk of femicide. Yet, the impact of participation in adversarial and collaborative family court proceedings on femicide has rarely been theorized. This gap is closed by the conflict theory described in the following pages.

The deductive conflict theory of separation-associated femicide created by Ellis (2017) is described in the following four propositions:

1. The risk of femicide varies with the intensity of conflict between the separating parties;
2. The intensity of conflict between them varies with the recency of separation and participation in proceedings aimed at settling separation-associated conflicts;
3. Participation in collaborative proceedings decreases and participation in adversarial proceedings increases the intensity of conflict—mutually hostile feelings—between participants;
4. Therefore, the risk of femicide will be greater among recently separated couples participating in adversarial proceedings.

Empirical support for this theory includes findings describing why participation in adversarial family court proceedings increases the intensity of conflict (p. 510), that such participation significantly increases the risk of femicide (p. 512), and that participation in collaborative proceedings such as separation/divorce mediation significantly decreases the risk of femicide (p. 512).

Two practice implications may be derived from the theory and findings described here. One, because it is a risk factor for femicide, DVDR investigators should collect information on participation in adversarial separation and divorce proceedings by past victims of femicide. Two, DVDR advisory group members should recommend participation in collaborative family court proceedings for contemporary mothers—victims of coercive control and MPV who are contemplating separation/divorce.

An unknown number of women are assaulted by their male partners prior to their participation in legal separation and divorce proceedings, but after communicating their firm decisions to end the relationship. MPV is used to prevent them from leaving or to persuade them to return if they have already left (Mahoney, 1991). Separation assaults and femicides cannot be explained by the Ellis theory because they are perpetrated before participation in adversarial family court proceedings. The coercively controlling behavior of male partners is a potent source of recurring conflicts between male and female intimate partners who don't simply endure but resist male partner control. The conflict-control theory created by Thibaut and Kelley (1959) can be used today to identify which male partners are most likely to perpetrate femicide and why.

Two types of control are identified by Thibaut and Kelley (1985). The first one is behavior control (pp. 103–104). Male partners exercising behavior control make it desirable for female partners to change their behaviors when they change their own behavior. Here, outcomes are determined by interaction between intimate partners.

The second one is fate control (Thibaut & Kelley, 1985, pp. 102–103). Male partners exercising fate control get female partners to do or not do what they want them to regardless of what their female partners do, want to do, or not do, So, when fate-controlling male partners themselves experience fate control by female partners who leave them, regardless of pleas for them to stay and promises to change, they are now experiencing fate control by female partners that have lifelong consequences (depression, loneliness, abandonment, and poverty) that are unbearable (Bornstein, 2008). Rage-motivated femicide is a futile means of restoring male partner fate control.

Of course, participation in adversarial family court proceedings and experiencing fate control are only two of the many factors identified in the other theories described in this chapter. Researchers Graham et al. (2022) claim to have created a theory or model that does a better or best job of explaining femicide because it integrates explanatory factors included in the feminist, evolutionary, and conflict theories described here.

Social Ecological

Gender, power, and control are central to the gendered theory of femicide described by Graham et al. (2002) in their Table 1. They are also central to the patriarchy theory included among the theories of nonfatal violence described in the first part of this chapter. Graham et al., go beyond the patriarchy/feminist theory referred to earlier in two ways. First, by identifying it as a radical feminist theory rather than a liberal feminist theory in which gender role socialization in families is the source of gender inequality and the oppression of women by men. Second, they identify a variety of feminist theories that identify factors not referred to in the feminist/patriarchy theory of nonfatal violence, such as "backlash, exposure reduction, intersectionality, self-defense, economic marginalization" (Graham et al., 2002, Table 1). All the risk and protective factors located at individual, relationship, community, and society levels in the Social Ecological Model (SEM theory) described on page 423 are gendered. In gendered theories of femicide, perpetrators are always male.

The Graham et al. (2022) gender SEM theory or model is designed for nonfatal and fatal violence prevention. The means to this end is the inclusion of "An array of individual, relationship, community and societal risk and protective factors in the SEM." These factors, and interactions among them, can increase or decrease the risk of violence perpetration by intimate partners. In their description of these factors, the perpetration of violence changes to the perpetration of intimate partner homicide (IPH).

Individual-level factors include substance use/abuse, mental illness, poverty, and age (being young). Relationship status includes "current or former partner." Community-level factors include the ability of communities to effectively mobilize or regulate local crime (i.e., collective efficacy), residing in rural communities, the availability of IPV supports and services, and firearm policies. Societal level factors include levels of discrimination by race, social class, gender, and ethnicity.

The attempt to facilitate the prevention of femicide by integrating different theoretical perspectives from which interventions can be derived is commendable. At the same time, their integrated SEM elicits these concerns. One, some factors central to the theories they attempt to integrate are not identified in it. For example, conflict is included as a relationship factor in the Heise (2011) ecological theory, and male partner sexual jealousy and possessiveness are central to the Daly and Wilson evolutionary psychological theory, but they are not included among the nine "gendered individual factors" they identify.

Two, a pattern of coercive control is identified as a reliable predictor of femicide in the eight-stage theory of femicide and feminist/patriarchal theories but is not included among the nine gendered individual risk factors in the SEM theory.

Three, DVDR recommendations can be derived from the SEM theory, but they do not have the capacity, resources, or legislative mandate to make recommendations aimed at changing many of the societal or community relationships identified in it. However, one of the major contributions of the SEM theory is that it identifies both risk and protective factors for femicide. Consequently, the effectiveness of the recommendations DVDRs can and do make can be increased by taking both risk and protective factors at the individual level, and the victim-perpetrator relationship at the gendered relationship level into account in making them.

A review of the homicide cases described in DVDR Annual Reports reveals that separation and infidelity are frequently found risk factors for femicides perpetrated by males against their female partners. Including factors identified in the social evolutionary theory created by Daly and Wilson (1988) would help increase its explanatory power, and the range of recommendations DVDR advisory group members can derive from it. Notwithstanding this contribution, recommendations derived from theories of femicide may not be appropriate for understanding and deriving recommendations aimed at preventing femicide-suicides.

FEMICIDE-SUICIDE

The inclusion of a femicide-suicide theory is warranted by findings indicating that femicide-suicides account for about 30% of all the homicide cases reviewed by DVDRs, and sometimes include children as victims (DVDRC Annual Report, 2019–2020, p. 13; Ellis et al., 2015), and between 18% and almost 40% of the 639 IPFs investigated by Sorrentino et al. (2022) were femicide-suicides. In many of the homicide-suicide cases described in DVDR Annual Reports, cases in which male perpetrators kill their heterosexual female partners, and then kill themselves immediately afterward are defined as homicides. The 639 femicide-suicides investigated by Sorrentino et al. (2022), are defined as femicides.

Evolutionary Psychological

In the evolutionary psychological theory created by Daly and Wilson (1988, p. 205), femicide-suicide is conceived of as a "two-edged sword" used most frequently when a female partner is suspected of infidelity or decides to end the relationship, and an extremely possessive, jealous and coercively controlling male partner male partner who believes that killing her to demonstrate his dominance, is "no more disastrous than losing her (and sometimes children) by desertion" (p. 219). In these cases, the manner of death is femicide, and the causes they identify are despair, desperation, and spite reflected in the statement, "I can't live without you (suicide), and no one else will live with you (femicide)" (Campbell, 1992, p. 99; Wilson & Daly, 1992, p. 89). The cause identified by this theory may call for domestic death review recommendations aimed at participation in suicide-prevention treatment programs provided by mental healthcare agencies.

Ecological

In an archival study conducted by Sorrentino et al. (2022), ecological theory was used to explain why 639 male intimate partners killed themselves after killing their female partners. Ecological theory was used to identify seven risk factors at the individual level, including previous MPV, substance abuse, and mental or physical illness. Previous couple violence, presence of children or stepchildren, the motives of jealousy, inability to accept separation or divorce, conflicts, mental illness of perpetrator and victim, and previous couple violence were included as relationship factors. The two contextual or situational risk factors identified by these researchers are the use of a gun and previous requests for help by the victim.

Four statistically significant predictors of femicide-suicide were found. They were conflicts, jealousy, occupation (law enforcement members who possess firearms), and an age gap—perpetrators were seven or more years older than victims.

Two of their findings are noteworthy. One, "law enforcement members are more at risk of committing homicide-suicide against their female intimate partners than their civilian counterparts." Two, among civilians, those who use guns to kill their intimate partners are most likely to commit suicide afterward.

Recommendations DVDRs can derive from the findings reported by Sorrentino et al. (2022) include health training for police officers and banning the possession of guns by male partners convicted of perpetrating criminal violence against their female intimate partners. On the other hand, DVDRs will not be able to derive recommendations grounded in data on protective factors for femicide-suicide because they were not identified by these researchers.

Moreover, if the risk factors for homicide-suicides perpetrated by firearm-possessing male partners in their sample more closely resemble risk factors for male intimate partners who commit suicide only than they are for male partners who commit homicide only (Humphrey, 1980), then perhaps DVDR recommendations aimed at preventing homicide-suicide should be aimed at preventing suicide instead of homicide. The thesis that homicide-suicides may be part of "the evolving process of suicide" (p. 106) was not tested in this study because comparisons with male partner homicide only and male partner suicide only cases were not made.

LESSONS LEARNED

First, DVDR recommendations grounded in theories of nonfatal MPV and femicide are likely to be more effective in preventing femicide than recommendations that are not derived from theories. Second, theories of femicide are more likely to reveal the dynamics underlying femicide than theories of male partner nonfatal violence. Third, theories of femicide are more likely to reveal the dynamics underlying femicide-suicide than theories of femicide. Fourth, SEM theory and femicide/patriarchy theory appear to be the only ones that can explain both nonfatal MPV and femicide. Five, theory is practically important.

4

✛

Research

SAMPLE SELECTION

The process of selecting empirical research studies began with a review of two sources of information. One is search engines (Google Scholar, PsycINFO, PubMed, Scopus). Two is journals (*Homicide Studies, Injury Epidemiology, Trauma Violence and Abuse, Violence Against Women and Family Violence*) in which publications on FRTs, DVDRCs, and DHRs have been published. Search terms used were "fatality review teams" and "evaluating the impact of fatality review teams on femicide." Searches revealed many repeat empirical research publications (e.g., Bugega et al., 2015; Jones et al., 2022), and descriptions of what domestic violence death reviews do and why they do it published in Annual Reports by DVDRs.

The searches identified here yielded a total of 1,406 records. DVDRs focusing on domestic violence-related homicides involving intimate partners as victims, accounted for 10% (n=146) of them. Other records (e.g., mass murder, SARS, COVID, car accidents) accounted for 84% of the records. The remaining 6% focused on child/youth, elder, and overdose fatalities. Of the 146 DVDRs focusing on intimate partner homicides, only four studies met the selection criterion of directly or indirectly assessing their impact on femicide.

FINDINGS

Findings based on an analysis of these four studies are presented in Table 4.1.

EVALUATION

Findings presented in Table 4.1 reveal that researchers who selected different samples, used different study designs, different analytic methods, and conducted their studies in different countries found DVDRs had no impact on femicide.

In interpreting the findings reported in Table 4.1, the primary objectives of the researchers whose studies are included should be considered. For example, the stated objective of Bugega et al. (2015) was to conduct "an international comparison of D/FVDRs and their core elements [in high income countries] to inform the establishment of D/FVDRs in low-income countries . . . where violence is the leading cause of death" (p. 179). Jones et al. (2022, pp. 1, 11) conducted a study aimed at "improving DVDR processes [and] assessing the the impact of DVFR recommendations" on a number of outcomes including domestic homicides. Montanez et al. (2023) investigated "the impact of policies and programs—including DV fatality review teams—on female-victim intimate partner homicide rates in 67 counties in Florida" (p. 253). Boughton's (2021) objective was "to critically analyze both the principles and the operation of DHRs in England and Wales" (p. 23).

A review of these studies reveals that Montanez et al. (2020) were the only researchers for whom assessing the impact of policies and programs, including FRTs, on homicide was the primary objective of their research project. This project elicited the following four comments.

One, the dependent variable (outcome) in their study was homicide rates per 100,000 persons aged 15 years and older. The source of their data was FBI Supplementary Homicide Reports (SHR) for the years 1996–2018 for 67 Florida counties. Knowing the data source is important because policy recommendations based SHR data in Florida are more likely to be valid if SHR rates of homicide were the same as, or similar to, homicide rates reported by police forces in Florida. However, Pizzaro and Zeoli (2011) found "notable discrepancies" between police data and SHR data with respect to rates of homicide in Newark, New Jersey.

Two, all or almost all FRTs refer to advisory group recommendations made to community-based organizations and agencies as interventions that will make a positive contribution toward preventing family violence and femicide. However, the mere presence/absence of an FRT in a county is not a valid measure of its impact on femicide. The impact of recommendations on homicide is a more valid measure, but it was not reported.

Three, many murders are prevented—become attempted murders—with timely and effective medical intervention. This happens so frequently as to result in attempted murders being recorded five times more frequently than murders (Dobson, 2002), but attempted murders

Table 4.1. Impact of Domestic Violence Death Reviews on Femicide

Author/date	Study Design[a]		Subject Selection[b]		Data Collection[c]			Data Analysis[d]		Findings
	Cross.	Long.	Pop.	Non-prob.	Obs.	Int.	Rec.	Qua.	Quant.	
Montanez et al. 2023	X		X				X			No impact
Jones et al. 2022	X			X			X		X	No impact
Bugega et al. 2015	X			X	X		X	X	X	No impact
Houghton 2019	X			X	X	X	X			No impact

[a]Cross-sectional/longitudinal
[b]Non-probability sample
[c]Observation/interview/records
[d]Quantitative/qualitative
[e]Found no impact or findings reported suggested no impact very likely (Boughton, 2021)

are not included in FBI Supplementary Homicide Reports. Consequently, the possibility that differences in homicide rates in Florida counties are mainly due to differences in access to hospitals with emergency wards and/or emergency response services cannot be ruled out as an explanation for why they have lower rates of homicide. In other words, higher rates for homicide in counties with FRTs than in counties with Coordinated Community Response (CCR) may have been found because access to hospitals and emergency medical services was far greater in CCR counties than in FRT counties.

Four, six "Theoretical frameworks . . . used in the explanation of IPH" are described on pages 257 and 258 (Montanez et al., 2020) but none of them are used by the authors to explain why FRTs do not have an impact on homicide rates in the counties in which they were located, and/or why CCR) counties have significantly lower rates of homicide than counties in which CCRs are not present.

Several interesting points relevant to the link between CCRs, on the one hand, and family violence and femicide on the other, are raised by these findings. First, as a "community-based response by multiple agencies that have the safety of battered women as their chief concern" is the primary purpose of both FRTs and CCRs in Florida, why were CCRs more effective than FRTs in achieving this shared primary purpose?

Second, findings reported by researchers who conducted "large scale, federally funded, multisite studies" comparing "coordinated" and "comparison" communities found a "lack of violence reduction" in all of them (Garner & Maxwell, 2009). In other words, like FRTs in Florida, CCRs had no discernible impact on decreasing family violence in the jurisdiction in which they were located.

Notwithstanding these comments, researchers Montanez et al. (2020), are to be commended for conducting a research project where, for the first time in over 25 years, assessing the impact of FRTs on femicide was the primary objective of an empirical research project.

A multisite empirical research project on femicide prevention was started by researchers at Yale and Michigan State universities but FRTs are not part of it (Holmes & Backes, 2016). The absence of FRTs in the multisite US Department of Justice–funded Domestic Violence Homicide Prevention Demonstration Initiative (DVHPDI) appears to be grounded in the hypothesis that programs using criminal justice system interventions such as the Newburyport High-Risk Team Response Model (Rosenfeld, 2022) are likely to be more effective in preventing femicide than FRTs which tend not to prioritize criminal justice system interventions. As FRTs were not included as a DVHPDI initiative, findings reported by Prevention Demonstration researchers will not actually test this hypothesis.

Findings reported by DVHPDI researchers in Yale and Michigan State universities cannot be reviewed because the research is ongoing.

The primary objective of the study conducted by Bugega et al. (2015, p. 179) was to compare domestic violence/family violence death reviews (D/FVDRs) in five developed, high-income countries to establishing D/FVDRs in low- and middle-income countries "where violence is a leading cause of death." All 25 of the D/FVDRs in their sample included "a reduction in deaths" as a goal of the review process. Two of the findings they reported are noteworthy.

First, none of the 25 D/FVDRs reported a reduction in deaths (Bugega et al., 2015, p. 185). Second, while "a reduction in deaths and strengthening service systems" were found to be common goals of D/FVDRs, "success was only reported with respect to the latter" (p. 179).

Two explanations for their findings are provided. First, compared with service systems, a reduction in deaths is "a more concrete and measurable outcome." Does this mean D/FVDRs are more likely to achieve objectives such as "strengthening service systems" because they are more abstract and difficult to measure and consequently more likely to be achieved?

Two, they state that D/FVDRs are "only one component of a larger set of reforms that may be necessary to contribute to any reduction in deaths and [consequently] isolating their independent contribution is difficult" (Bugega et al., 2015, p. 185). This is probably true, but other co-present reforms can be controlled—taken into account statistically—by researchers who use multivariate statistical procedures to analyze data on topics such as homicide and suicide. Studies conducted by Azrael et al. (2013) and Montanez et al. (2020) are examples. Note that Montanez et al.could have investigated counties in Florida five years before and after the establishment of FRTs in selected counties taking into account other reforms that may have been implemented in them between year one and year five.

Findings reported by Bugega et al. (2015) "raise the question of whether or not the aim of [preventing femicide] may be an inappropriate measure of the impact of D/FVDRs because it essentially sets them up to fail to meet their stated aims." One practice implication derived from this response is not to include preventing femicide as a purpose of D/FVDRs. More generally, the finding that D/FVDRs do not result in the reduction of deaths in higher-income countries raises a question about the wisdom of establishing them in lower-income countries where the rates of violence are between 10 and 20 times higher (e.g., El Salvador 13.8, Venezuela 10.7, Central African Republic, 10.6) than the rates in the United States, Canada, and the United Kingdom. Moreover, Femicide Observatories (FOs) are already established in several middle- and low-income countries such as Venezuela, Trinidad, and Lebanon (UNODC, 2023, pp. 43, 75). Perhaps a rationale for establishing DVDRs as an alternative or supplement to FOs could accompany proposals to establish DVDRs in them.

Findings reported by Pronyk et al. (2022) strongly suggest a compelling rationale for establishing DVDRs in lower-income countries such as Honduras, El Salvador, and Uruguay, with the highest rates of femicide (United Nations, 2022). The rationale would state that DVDRs are more likely than FOs to promote gender equality by linking training or education on gender equity with micro-loans for local projects promoting the independence of women and the economies of families. Findings based on a randomized trial conducted in rural South Africa revealed that this intervention reduced intimate partner violence—a risk factor for femicide—by 55%.

The primary objective of the study conducted by Jones et al. (2022) was to review research on FRT recommendations in a sample of 11 diverse FRTs. Their search via 11 search engines using 14 key term searches yielded 22,531 records. The 11 FRTs in their sample were the only ones that met their 14-item selection criteria. Like Bugega et al. (2015) these researchers found no evidence supporting the FRT thesis that reviewing homicide cases and making recommendations prevents femicide.

Four reasons for the failure of FRTs to prevent femicide were stated. First, recommendations were not implemented. Second, recommendations were not mandatory and those that were implemented voluntarily were not tracked. These are good reasons for failure. The third reason, "difficulty of forging a causal link between the work of reviews, their recommendations and the incidence of deaths" (p. 11), is not a good one because it would also apply to forging a causal link between recommendations and other outcomes of FRT recommendations, such as system change, educating practitioners and increasing public awareness. Applying the criterion of causality would tend to make FRTs redundant.

Moreover, random controlled studies are not the only method of establishing a causal relation between recommendations and the reduction of deaths. For example, a causal relation can be established in cases where (a) recommendations precede femicides (b) are strongly associated with femicides, and (c) a change in recommendations—say an FRT ceases to operate because of a lack of funding—increases the rate of femicide.

Notwithstanding these comments, Jones et al. (2022) made a positive contribution to the corpus of knowledge on DVDRs and DHRs in three ways. First, they drew attention to the difficulty of establishing a causal relation between risk factors and femicide (Roehl & Guertin, 2000, p. 174). Second, they reported findings indicating "there was little evidence of whether recommendations were implemented."

Third, by supporting Storer et al. (2013), recommendations such as (a) using naming and rewarding agencies who collaborate with each other and coordinate their interventions (b) providing government "innovation grants" to those who act in this way, and (c) extending DVDR or DHR recommendations "across different agencies" instead of being mainly targeted at individual organizations and agencies" (p. 13).

Empirical evidence supporting the Jones et al. (2022) finding and the Storer et al. (2013) recommendations was cited by a group of "survivors, advocates & activist" (SAA) researchers in Canada who published the results of a study investigating "the Implementation of Domestic Violence Death Review Committee Recommendations in 2014." Specifically, they investigated 169 recommendations made by the Ontario DVDRC to 21 different organizations and agencies between 2007 and 2011. Four of their most significant findings follow.

First, some organizations and agencies are far less likely to implement DVDRC recommendations than others. For example, the Ontario Association of Police Chiefs did not respond to any of the 19 recommendations made to them, and the First Nations Police did not respond to the two recommendations they received. The Canadian Psychiatric Associations, psychiatrists, and other mental health workers did not respond to any of the four recommendations they received, and the Ontario Association of Children's Aid Societies and Health Care Providers responded to only one of six DVDRC recommendations made to them, On the other hand, the Ministry of the Attorney General responded to all four of the recommendations, and the Ontario Women's Directorate responded to all 20 recommendations they received.

The pattern revealed by a review of DVDRC recommendations investigated by SAA researchers appears to be one in which mental healthcare and law enforcement professionals are least likely to respond to DVDR recommendations, and representatives of women's organizations and a government ministry responsible for "conduction litigation on behalf of all government ministries" are most likely to respond to them.

Second, many recommendations were aimed at promoting changes that were to be implemented by individual organizations and agencies or only within them. For example, DVDR recommendation (#16-2011/1) states: "social service/probation examine the potential requirement for intervention specifically designed for women perpetrators of violence and domestic violence." The "potential requirement" for social services and probation to collaborate and coordinate their interventions is not included in this recommendation. Another example, recommendation #16-2010/2 states, "Police training should include instruction on how to deal with resistant or reluctant victims of domestic violence." Collaboration with advocates for victims in developing training courses for police officers was not included in this recommendation. Consequently, police officers are not trained to take the adverse consequences of cooperating with the police into account in how they respond to "reluctant or resistant victims."

Third, incentives for organizations and agencies who share information and promptly implement coordinated interventions are not included in any of the 169 DVDR recommendations reviewed by SAA researchers.

Femicide rates may also be reduced by mandatory recommendations followed by the imposition of sanctions for failure to implement them in high-risk victimization cases. At the same time, agencies that fully implement recommendations in these cases may be rewarded for doing so by submitting their names to the media. This would be consistent with what FRTs operating in the shadow of a no-blame subculture would do.

Reflecting the different jurisdictions in which they are located, the 146 FRTs investigated by the researchers named in Table 4.1 are quite diverse with respect to their "structure, governance, case identification processes and inclusion criteria, review measures and outputs" (Bugega et al., 2015). They also differ with respect to the selection of advisory group chairs, whether the police or coroners are the source of the homicide cases they review, and whether the homicide cases reviewed are "live" or adjudicated (Cook et al., 2023). At the same time, qualitative researcher Watt (2010) discovered that all the DVDRs she studied faced the same "critical tensions." The four studies she investigated also share several attributes such as a no-blame subculture, nonmandatory recommendations, multiagency composition, and other attributes and proclivities known only to qualitative researchers who go inside the Black Box of DVDRs to actually observe their secret deliberations.

In 2022, Rowlands published an article titled "Inside the Black Box: Domestic Homicide Reviews as a Source of Data." In this publication, Rowlands argued for researchers to go inside the secret Black Box of the DHR process of reviewing homicide cases because the results of such studies would yield data that was important for conducting research on femicide, homicide, and other health-related issues.

Three years earlier, Boughton (2021, chap. 5) went inside the Black Box of the DHR process of reviewing homicide cases, but not for the reason stated by Rowlands. Boughton's reason for entering it was to "critically evaluate the DHR process in England and Wales." To this end, she conducted a qualitative research project in which data were collected from three sources: interviews with 34 advisory group members, observation of six DHRs, and reviews of 48 private documents on DHR deliberations.

In her dissertation, Boughton (2021, chap. 8) states, "This research has not explored whether DHRs have helped to reduce the rate of homicides." However, the findings she reports led her to conclude that parts of the DHR process make DHRs "unfit for the purposes" they were designed to achieve, including the purpose of preventing femicide. Lack of accountability and culpability is the first part of the process. The failure of recommendations to make a positive contribution toward the achievement of stated objectives is the second part. Lack of accountability and culpability are grounded in the fact that DHRs operate in the shadow of a no-blame subculture, and the failure of recommendations is caused by the fact that DHR recommendations are not mandatory.

Boughton's (2021) dissertation is replete with findings based on interviews with advisory group members and observations of DHRs that support her radical not-fit-for-purpose conclusion. In Chapter 5, Boughton asks, how can DHRs operating in the shadow of a no-blame subculture, and making nonmandatory recommendations "be considered fit-for-purpose if there is lack of transparency concerning the implementation and subsequent monitoring of recommendations"?

An evaluation of FRTs conducted by AI (i.e., ChatGPT) yielded the following even more radical conclusion: "Without robust mechanisms for continued investment for evaluating effectiveness, it can be challenging to justify continued investment in [FRTs]." Caveat: The ChatGPT conclusion was grounded in empirical research, but it is not included in Table 4.1 because of the absence of information on the study design (longitudinal or cross-sectional), size, type of sample, and how the data were analyzed.

Some years prior to Boughton's research, Watt (2010) entered the Black Box of FRTs to collect data for her dissertation, *Domestic Violence Fatality Review Teams: Collaborative Efforts to Prevent Intimate Partner Violence.*

The major reason for not including Watt's research in Table 4.1 is that it does not yield findings on the impact of FRTs on femicide. Still, it is included in this chapter for two reasons. First, Watt (2010) found that all 35 FRTS in the sample shared the goal of promoting system change, but "None of them linked it with preventing femicide as a goal." This finding supports the practice implication of excluding femicide prevention as one of the purposes of DVDRs.

Second, the great variety across the 35 FRTs she studied coexists with five shared "critical tensions."

One of them is the tension between "understanding vs action" (Watt, 2010, p. 66). Understanding refers to the prioritization of "increasing awareness and knowledge of risk factors contributing to femicide and gaps in the system response to it." Action refers to the prioritization of active involvement of FRTs in monitoring and implementing recommendations. Understanding and action are conceived of as different means used to achieve the shared goal of promoting system change as an end in itself, not as a means of preventing femicide.

Findings indicating the achievement of system change did not result in a reduction of femicide (Visher et al., 2008), plus the absence of any reference to theorizing system change in the National Fatality Team

Conference Summit (1999), or any consideration of deriving recommendations from a theory of system change by the creators of FRTs, led Watt to argue for the creation of a theory of system change that would "provide domestic violence fatality review teams a framework for establishing, operating and evaluating these teams, and provided a conscious decision-making process to encourage a match between desired outcomes and the specific strategies that would encourage these outcomes" (Watt, 2010, p. 85).

The absence of systems theory in the studies included in Table 4.1 is noteworthy. The absence of any reference to protective factors for family violence and femicide in them and the 47 FRT reports reviewed by Pow et al. (2015) is equally noteworthy.

The risk factors revealed by death review investigators usually include proximal (situational) risk factors for lethality such as arguments and separation. However, the finding that some, but not all arguments or separations result in femicide requires (a) the collection of data on both aggravating and protective factors by domestic violence death by review investigators (Block, 2000; Markham, 1993; Sowan, 2023), and (b) grounding advisory group recommendations in both risk and protective factors.

In the enumerated risk factors for lethality published in DVDR Annual Reports, actual or intended separation initiated by intimate female partners is included among the top two or three. Enumerated lists of protective factors for family violence and femicide for female partners contemplating separation or divorce are not included in any of them.

Separating is a process that ends with a final decision to stay or leave. Many women who were killed by their current or former male partners contacted the police and/or community-based organizations and agencies whose mandates included preventing family violence and femicide. An unknown number of them who were beaten equally often or seriously injured and coercively controlled to the same degree by their current or former male partners did not contact any service agency other than the emergency ward of a hospital and were not killed by their current or former male partners. What protected them from femicide (Block, 2000)?

The absence of empirical research findings comparing rates of femicide among stayers and leavers for at least one year following the end of an intimate partner relationship is a gap that can be filled by DVDRs who (a) collect data on risk and protective factors and (b) select one or two researchers with expertise on estimating the probability and risk of family violence and femicide as members of their multi-agency advisory groups.

For example, data collected on female partners who were (a) raped while intimate partners were living together (b) raped by their intimate partners after separating, and (c) not raped while they were living together, the probability they will be raped after separating given they were raped while they were living together was estimated to be 35.4% by the author using a relatively simple Bayesian theorem (Silver, 2012, pp. 240–43). In this case "not being raped while living together" was the protective factor. If attempted murder is substituted for rape, then "attempted murder via strangulation did not occur while living together" would be a protective factor if it decreased the probability of femicide.

Estimates of the probability of rape and attempted murders could then be used to derive recommendations aimed at preventing the perpetration of these serious crimes against separating and separated women. A researcher who is also a member of a DHR Panel found DHR reports to be "a rich source of data for social science researchers" (Rowlands, 2022). Instead of providing data for other researchers to make these estimates, DVDRs could do it for themselves to achieve the objectives for which they were originally created.

RECOMMENDATIONS

A novel alternative to changing the composition of DVDRs is suggested by the longitudinal, comparative *Chicago Women's Health Risk Study* (Block, 2000).

The goal of this study was homicide prevention. The objective was "to give nurses, patrol officers, and other primary support people the information they need to help women who are experiencing violence [by a current or former partner] to lower the risk or life-threatening injury or death." The specific purpose was to "identify risk factors for life-threatening injury or death in situations in which an intimate partner is physically abusing women." Manifestly, the goal and main purpose of the Chicago study are similar to those of DVDRs.

Applied to DVDRs, the Block model would require the location of a research DVDR (RDVDR) in states in the United States, provinces in Canada, and regions in England and Wales. Within each of these larger locations, researchers would select all current or adjudicated femicide and attempted femicide cases reported by the police and/or coroners/medical examiners occurring in year one in a high risk of intimate partner violence in two sites. One is the "hottest spots" for family violence in a city identified in police hotspot maps. Two is a rural county with high family violence rates located some distance from a city. In each of these jurisdictions, a "clinic/hospital sample" of all women aged 18 and older who visited hospitals and clinics for any reason in year one would be selected. Women in this sample would be administered a three-item screening instrument.

Women who are screened in as well as those who were screened out would be interviewed twice—once in year one and at the end of year two—by RDVDR research staff who would respect the safety and privacy standards of the clinics and hospitals. Interviewing women in both groups will yield two outcomes.

First, it would ensure that "women who are at high risk for femicide or life-threatening injuries but unknown to be at risk by any helping agency" are included in the comparison sample. Two, aggravating and protective factors would be revealed to researchers.

Women in both groups would also be asked to complete a "past year one" questionnaire that includes questions about risk and demographic factors, and a "calendar history/story" starting from the date of the first interview. The history/story will include coercive controlling incidents, suicidal proclivities, substance abuse, and mental and physical health problems that occurred during the past year.

Qualitative story/history data could be analyzed using N Vivo software to identify themes and patterns. Appropriate multivariate statistics may be used to estimate the probability of family violence and femicide and risk estimates for these outcomes. Recommendations aimed at preventing femicide and life-threatening injuries against women facing the highest risk of experiencing these outcomes could be made to DVDRs located in the jurisdiction of the RDVDR. An RDVDR Report would be disseminated to DVDRs at the end of every second year. A five-year evaluation report would be published online at the end of the period. Implementing the Block research model will help make DVDRs more fit for the purpose of preventing femicide and life-threatening injuries against female intimate partners.

A less ambitious model would help make DVDRs more fit for achieving these purposes including new legislation, and new statutory guidelines. New legislation will make (a) DVDR recommendations mandatory for "high risk for femicide and attempted femicide victims," and (b) DVDRs independent of the office of coroners/medical examiners or other government ministries and bureaucracies.

New statutory guidelines for DVDRs would:

- Make preventing femicide and attempted femicide the primary objective of DVDRs;
- Mandate coordination among family violence prevention organizations and agencies;
- Require the inclusion of at least two researchers as members of DVDR advisory groups;

- Require an independent evaluation of large city, state, provincial, and regional DVDRs at least once every five years, and publish the results of their evaluations online;
- Require the publication of Annual Reports that make a positive contribution toward increasing public awareness and understanding of lethal and nonlethal violence against women by reporting the prevalence of femicide, the circumstances in which femicides occurred, and the dynamics underlying them.

LESSONS LEARNED

One, very few empirical studies on the impact of DVDRs on femicide have been published. Two, different researchers in different countries, using different samples and methods of analysis found that DVDRs have no impact on femicide rates. Three, positive contributions to the corpus of knowledge on DVDRs have been made by qualitative and quantitative research.

5

✛

Implications for Practice

In this chapter, implications for practice are derived from investigations of attributes shared by DVDRCs in Canada, FRTs in the United States, and DHR panels in Britain. Other attributes are unique to DVDRCs and FRTs located in the offices of coroners and medical examiners, respectively. DHRs are not located in the office of coroners in the United Kingdom.

The starting point for the death investigations conducted by many FRTs and DVDRCs is a death certificate signed by a coroner or medical examiner in which the cause and manner of the death being investigated are identified. Cause refers to how and why death occurred (e.g., strangulation). Manner refers to a domestic (intimate partner) violence-related homicide. Usually, coroners are required to investigate specified types of death such as deaths that appear to be the result of homicide or suicide. Postmortem is the method used to determine homicide as the cause and manner of death. Cases found to be domestic violence-related homicides are submitted to DVDRs for review. DVDRs of homicide cases are governed by rules and regulations for the OCC or medical examiners. That is to say, DVDR teams and committees operate in the shadow of the rule of coroners.

CORONIAL RULE

Coronial rule refers to the authority of chief coroners to appoint chairs of advisory groups; accept or reject jury recommendations; enforce compliance with rules regulating the investigation of past domestic

violence-related homicides to prevent future homicides in similar circumstances, requiring confidentiality or privacy, and producing high-quality
death investigations by coroners and forensic pathologists.

In many counties in the United States, police officers (sheriff-coroners)
are legally authorized to sign death certificates. In domestic homicide
cases involving police officers as perpetrators, conflicts of interest may
be settled by signing death certificates in which homicides are found to
be nonculpable, even in cases where forensic pathologists found them to
be culpable homicides (Los Angeles Times Editorial Board, 2022). These
homicides are not reviewed by FRTs and consequently, recommendations
aimed at preventing them cannot be made by FRTs.

Two practice implications flow from the preceding paragraph. One,
legislation expanding the coronial rule includes lobbying for advisory
group recommendations aimed at preventing femicide by high-risk male
partners to be made mandatory. In Australia, coroner recommendations
are mandatory in some jurisdictions. Two, separate the job of coroner
from the job of police officers in jurisdictions where sheriffs are also
coroners.

Coronial rule varies in its effectiveness in different jurisdictions, or the
same jurisdiction at different times. Investigation of the effectiveness of
coronial rule is important not only because it results in poor-quality post-
mortems, but also because it results in poor-quality recommendations
made by DVDR teams and committees that review these cases.

STUDY DESIGN

The objective of investigating past femicides to predict and prevent future
femicides in similar circumstances calls for a retrospective-prospective
study design. Retrospective refers to investigating risk factors for past
femicides. Prospective refers to investigating the impact of risk factors for
past femicides on future femicides. This is the study design used by FRTs
in the United States and DVDRCs in Canada. As the cases investigated by
them are usually adjudicated cases, there will be a gap of between three
and five years between past and present femicides. Consequently, any
social changes (e.g., COVID, funding cuts to family violence prevention
agencies, increased unemployment rates) influencing the prevalence of
homicide or femicide must be taken into account (controlled statistically)
in determining the independent effect of the presence of risk factors for
past femicides on future femicides. In her "Commentary on a Websdale"
article, Hauser (2005) goes so far as to state that this approach involves
comparing oranges and apples because future femicides (apples) occur
when "social conditions, intervention strategies and social policies are

different from those present in past femicides (oranges)" (p. 1201). In other words, the past is not invariably prologue.

One practice implication that can be derived from this real possibility is for DVDRs to collect data on past adjudicated homicides and attempted femicides during the past two years. Other things being equal, the shorter the time between collecting data on risk factors for past homicides and using the data to predict future homicides, the greater their positive predictive power.

DEFINITIONS

In the Santa Clara FRT, the Ontario DVDRC, and the West Berkshire DHR, intentional killings of females by their male intimate partners are defined as homicides. For example, authors of the Ontario DVDRC 2019–2020 Annual Report found "100% of the primary victims [of homicide] were women and 91% of the perpetrators were men" (p. 8). This finding is supported by national findings indicating that between 2007 and 2001 "no men were killed by their separated or divorced spouses, but an average of eighty wives were killed by their husbands" (Sinha, 2013, p. 14). Ellis, Stuckless, and Smith (2015) found almost all intimate partner homicide-suicides were perpetrated by males against female partners and sometimes their children.

Notwithstanding these findings, the murder and manslaughter of women by their male intimate partners are not defined as femicides— a concept that names the gender of perpetrators and victims. The practice implication of this finding is obvious—define the intentional killings of females by their male intimate partners as femicides in the Criminal Codes of States in the United States, Canada, and the United Kingdom.

DATA COLLECTION

"Garbage in, garbage out" is an idiom created by a computer programmer in the early 1960s. It has been used so frequently in evaluating studies conducted by empirical researchers generally, and researchers publishing books and articles on programs designed to solve social problems in particular, as to have acquired its own acronym, GIGO. In this segment, GIGO is being used only to draw attention to the importance of collecting data that may increase the ability of DVDRs to achieve their stated purposes, including the purpose of decreasing the risk of family violence and femicide.

Unfortunately, practice implications derived from a review of the link between data collection and the achievement of stated DVDR purposes are not reviewed here because few if any of them tracked their recommendations, and subsequently included their findings in Annual Reports (Dawson et al., 2016). Consequently, evidence of their impact remains "anecdotal"—a synonym for unreliable (UNODC, 2023, p. 38). Beyond anecdotal information, Chopra et al. (2022, p. 3094 found "the absence of information on trigger events, the under reporting of stalking—especially digital stalking—and interpersonal violence, and significant differences in relevant details in Reports by different DHRs."

The National Reviews Summit of FRTs (McHardy & Hofford, 1999) recommended the collection of data from 25 different formal and informal sources. The information on risk factors for lethality collected from these sources is obtained from proxy informants. For example, the Ontario DVDRC members review "confidential file information" provided by "a friend, co-worker, family member and/or, shelter staff, counsellor, Children's Aid Society, police reports."

Compared with data on the presence of risk factors for femicide (e.g., separation, substance abuse, coercive control, suicide attempts) disclosed by survivors of attempted murders and manslaughters, information provided by proxy informants is likely to be less reliable and valid because they (a) may not have witnessed the "trigger incident," (b) may not be aware of the presence of risk factors for victims, and/or may be reluctant to disclose them, such as their infidelity or substance abuse, (c) the best interest of proxies themselves may not be served by fully disclosing all the information they possess to the police, such as not reporting the violence in the presence of young children they witnessed to the police (Chopra et al., 2022; Glass et al., 2008; Santana et al., 1997; Zahn, 2003, p. 12).

Another concern, this one elicited by the collection of data from multiple sources, is that different sources may be privy to different kinds of information, and we do not know which source or sources are given the greatest weight in determining the importance of any given risk factor. As data from survivors of attempted femicides are likely to be one of the most valid and reliable sources of data on risk factors for domestic violence-related femicides (Zahn, 2003), correlations with survivor data could be used to determine the weight or importance of each of the 40 or more risk factors—or at least the "top 10"—found by the Ontario DVDRC.

Caveat: This strategy may help solve the weighting risk factor problem, but the positive contribution made to achieving system change by collecting data on victims and perpetrators from multiple community-based sources perpetrators and victims may have contacted or been involved with, may suffer when these agencies do not also share information with each other (UNODC, 2023, p. 34).

A third concern is that information from female intimate partner survivors of attempted murders is not collected by DVDR investigators.
Findings reported by Nicolaidis et al. (2003, p. 7) identify "frequent arguments" as a precursor or "trigger incident" for the attempted femicides
they experienced. Moreover, the complex dynamics underlying femicide
are more likely to be revealed by eliciting stories told by victims of attempted murder, than by interviewing proxies (Nicolaidis et al., 2003).
The dynamic found by these researchers—her decision to end the relationship because of the increasing frequency and intensity of the arguments, his pleading to get her back, and then finally the near-fatal attack
when he realized she really meant to leave him—was also found by
Dobash et al. (2007) and Winstock and Eisikovits (2008).

In many, if not most domestic violence-related femicide investigations, investigators look for and find "a history/frequency of domestic
violence." What they are less likely to look for, and consequently do not
find, is the recency of male partner violence prior to the femicide. Researcher Block (2000, p. 25) identified 30 days as the time of greatest risk
following separation, and Ellis, Stuckless, and Smith (2015, p. 42) found
74% of femicides occurred between two and six months following separation. However, attempts to murder partners by any means, especially via
strangulation and gunshots, at any time during the relationship are also
identified as important risk factors for femicide by researchers such as
Glass et al. (2008), Zahn (2003), and Zeoli et al. (2020).

The Dallas County and New Jersey FRTs are included among the
few that say they collect data from victims who experienced near-fatal
injuries. Collecting data on the recency of male partner violence before
perpetrating femicide, and on the attempted femicide of females by their
male partners at any time during their relationship is one of the practice
implications derived from the evidence and argument presented here.

Separation is included among the top two risk factors for femicide in
many DHRs. Data collected by investigators of past femicides are limited
to actual separations or plans to separate by female partners. Information
about other factors associated with separation that may increase the risk
of femicide is not collected. One of these factors is the number of times female partners leave and return to live with their violent, coercive controlling male partners (Anderson, 2003; Campbell et al., 1998). The practice
implication derived from this finding is for DVDR investigators to collect
information about the pattern of leaving and returning to coercively controlling, physically violent, and emotionally abusive male partners.

Finally, and perhaps most importantly, in the "domestic violence" literature, lethal and nonlethal violence by male intimate partners is defined
as the result of a "pattern of coercive controlling behavior" (National Network to End Domestic Violence, n.d.), but data on this potent precursor

of femicide are rarely collected by the major sources (coroners or police officers) of information about the homicides reviewed by DVDRs. Consequently, DVDR recommendations are not grounded in knowledge of either the process of some risk factors (e.g., separation) or patterns of coercive controlling behavior and physical violence.

For example, in October 2023, five persons, including three children, were shot to death, and another person was shot but not killed in Sault Saint Marie, a city located in northern Ontario. The perpetrator committed suicide. The police identified a prior arrest for intimate partner violence, and perpetrator free on bail as risk factors for the homicide-suicide. If and when this homicide-suicide case is reviewed by the Ontario DVDRC, recommendations aimed at preventing femicide are likely to be grounded exclusively in the number of separate risk factors present, instead of a pattern revealed by a latent trait analysis of all the risk factors identified using coercive controlling behavior as the latent trait (Myhill & Hohl, 2016, pp. 74–75).

Because of the seriousness of this domestic violence mass murder-suicide, the widespread publicity describing it, and the fact that the perpetrator was free on bail following his court appearance on a domestic violence charge when he committed the murders, an inquest is likely to be held on this case. At the inquest, women's advocates are likely to be given standing. From the inquest, jury members will learn about the dynamics underlying the murders, and that they were the endpoint of a pattern of coercive male partner control.

What is to be done? Collect stories about attempted femicides from victims who survived them. These data are more likely to reveal patterns and underlying dynamics than data collected from proxy informants interviewed by police officers or, administering instruments to them and checking off yes/no answers to the list of risk factors included in them.

Greater progress toward achieving the purpose of system change is also likely to be made if data on the frequency, duration, and results of contacting and becoming involved with agents of the criminal and family court systems, as well as organizations and agencies whose purposes include preventing family violence was also collected from survivors of attempted murders by DVDR investigators.

DATA ANALYSIS

Femicide is a complex problem. Predicting and preventing it is challenging, requiring sophisticated multivariate (many variables) statistical methods of analysis. These statistical analyses are not conducted by DV-DRCs. However, they do make a positive contribution toward increasing public awareness and education by publishing descriptions of the reality of different types of homicide, and relatively simple types of statistical analysis such as description of the frequency distribution of a single factor (e.g., 60% of the homicides occurred in a residence shared by the perpetrator and victim), or the link between two factors (e.g., 67% of the victims of homicide were separated). Some DVDRs also include information about trends such as the number of domestic violence homicide victims each year between 2007 and 2017.

The rationale for using relatively simple types of data analysis is that the findings presented in graphs, figures, and tables can be easily understood by readers of DVDR Annual Reports and segments submitted to the media. Good examples of Annual Reports that include a variety of easily understood graphs, histograms, tables, and figures were published by the Dallas County FRT, the Ontario DVDRC, the Florida FRT, and the Hawaii FRT. On the other hand, none of these methods of analysis are fit for the purpose of estimating the probability and risk of domestic violence of past or present related homicides.

Specifically, the data analytic methods used by DVDRs suffer from the fact that—unlike weather forecasters who routinely report the probability of precipitation, leaving it "up to people" to decide whether or not to plan a picnic—simpler methods of analysis do not estimate the probability of femicide in the presence of a risk factor (e.g., separation), leaving it up to female partners to stay or leave their coercively controlling abusive partners.

It is important for estimates of the probability of femicide to be separated from estimates of risk (odds ratios) because they can vary independently. For example, the probability that an abusive, depressed male will kill his female partner may be very high because he attempted to strangle her to death twice during the past year, but the risk may be very low—zero—because he is serving a life sentence for attempted murder in a penitentiary. On the other hand, the probability that a husband will kill his wife may be very low—he never physically abused or coercively controlled her during the twenty years they lived together—but the probability that he would kill her increased significantly when he became extremely depressed and suicidal after he was served with a notice of divorce that included a claim for sole custody of their two children by his wife.

One factor impeding the use of more technically sophisticated methods of statistical analysis to estimate probability and risk is that a larger number of homicides and homicide-suicides are not available for analysis. For example, between 1993 and 1997 the Santa Clara County FRT reviewed only 51 homicide and homicide-suicide cases, and between 2019 and 2021 only 21 cases were available for analysis by the Ontario DVDR serving a province that included 5,531,925 married couples and 858,523 divorced couples. A greater number of adjudicated cases would be made available for analysis if (a) murders and attempted murders were reviewed, and (b) all attempted murder and attempted murder cases occurring during a five-year period as was reviewed by advisory group members every sixth year. Homicide-suicides can be analyzed shortly after they occur because the perpetrators committed suicide. Consequently, these cases cannot be adjudicated.

A second factor impeding the use of enhanced methods of statistical analysis is the lack of expertise among DVDR advisory group members. Hiring consultants who possess the required expertise to conduct a study once every five years is one way of solving this problem. Selecting researchers with the required competence as DVDR advisory group members is another. These are two practice implications that can be derived from the evidence and argument presented here.

Advocates for DVDRs are likely to respond to the implementation of relatively sophisticated multivariate methods of statistical analyses on the grounds that they are not research bodies (e.g., Rowlands, 2022). However, they do make recommendations aimed at preventing family violence and femicide based on the collection and quantitative analysis of data on risk factors. The use of univariate (one variable) and bivariate (two variables) statistical analyses opens DHRs to the Coggin criticism that their investigations are "light touch investigations" (2008 DHR Report, p. 9, fn10). What Member of Parliament Coggins may be saying is that femicide is a complex problem, and recommendations aimed at preventing it should be grounded in findings from more sophisticated methods of statistical and qualitative analysis.

RISK FACTORS

The work of DVDRs—particularly DVDRCs and FRTs—is dominated by the search for risk factors for past femicides, advisory group deliberations about them, and deriving recommendations aimed at preventing them in the future. The risk factors they search for can be correlates, predictors, or causes of femicide (Murray et al., 2009). Risk factors are correlated when they are frequently linked with femicide, predictors when they are found to be present before femicide, and causes when changing the predictor changes the risk of femicide. Predictors yield recommendations aimed at addressing symptoms. Causes address factors underlying symptoms. None of the risk factors identified in FRTs and DVDRCs are causes of femicide.

The use of risk factors as predictors draws attention to problems that may arise where the top two risk factors for femicide—male partner violence and separation—are present but information collected by DVDR investigators does not reveal which came first. Did male partner violence lead to the decision to separate by the female partner, or did the violence occur after she told him she was leaving (Rezey, 2017)?

Problems associated with predicting femicide can also be traced to the failure to include the male partner's patterned use of coercive controlling tactics among the top two or three predictors of femicide (Hart, 2015). For example, 31 types of coercive controlling behavior are listed in the United Kingdom, Serious Crime Act (2015) but only one type—"Controls partner's activities"—is included among the bottom seven of the 22 risk factors listed in the statewide Florida FRT (2019). In the Ontario DVDRC (Annual Report, 2018, p. 15), two types of coercive controlling behavior are included among the bottom eight list of common risk factors.

Moreover, a review of DVDR Annual Reports, segments published in the media, and recommendations made to practitioners are dominated by the belief that the use of validated risk assessment instruments is the necessary and sufficient condition for effective risk management. Recommendations stating that the use of a risk assessment instrument—check marks on a sheet of paper—should be used in conjunction with, or as a supplement to, an understanding of the dynamics underlying family violence and femicide is conspicuous by its absence in DVDR Annual Reports.

Shiva (1997) and Hauser (2005) oppose the use of risk assessment instruments even as a supplement to understanding underlying dynamics because risk scores based upon check marks on a sheet of paper yield fragmented knowledge of battered women and their relationships.

Finally, it is important to note that some of the risk factors for femicide included in DVDR Annual Reports are "dynamic," meaning they can be changed by appropriate interventions (e.g., gender equality, school curricula that promote healthy relationships), others are "static" (e.g., the past experience of having a criminal record, skin color, and being abused and neglected as a child) cannot be changed, but the adverse effects and trauma caused by them may be changed.

One practice implication derived from the first finding is for FRTs and DVDRCs to collect and analyze data informed by one or more theories of femicide identifying dynamic causal risk factors. A second practice implication is for DVDR investigators to collect data on the timing of two of the most important dynamic precursors/risk factors for femicide—separation and male partner violence.

A review of the literature on femicide will reveal consensus on the finding that a coercive controlling pattern of male partner behavior preceding femicide is far more dangerous than- by implication- lists of incidents (Kelly & Johnson, 2008, p. 478). However, these researchers did not take the next step that was taken by Myhill and Hohl (2016). Myhill and Hohl conceived of coercive control as a "latent trait" that could be measured by the strength of its positive association with other measurable and modifiable risk factors, including physical violence (Graham-Kevan & Archer, 2008). The presence of this subset of risk factors results in patterns of male partner behavior that increase the probability of femicide.

The practice implication derived from the findings reported by Myhill and Hohl (2016) is for DVDR teams, committees, and panels to (a) use coercive control as the latent trait, and (b) hire consultants to conduct a latent trait analysis of this multidimensional construct. For the Santa Clara County FRT and Ontario DVDRC, the 17 and 41 risk factors identified in their respective Annual Reports would be included in a latent trait analysis.

Chopra et al. (2022) investigated data from all 363 DHR cases involving "past or present intimate partners as perpetrators and victims." A latent trait analysis using coercive control as the latent trait may reveal that coercive control was consistently associated with psychological abuse, physical abuse, injuries, threats, attempts to isolate victim and damage to property/possessions (Chopra et al., 2021, Table 2). Coercive control is likely to be consistently associated with a different set of risk factors when the time frame is confined to "Previous 2 months before homicide." During this period, the six risk factors for homicide are: separated or about to be, stalking/harassment, new intimate relationship, fear for her safety, involvement with primary care health services and the police, faced barriers to housing and services.

PROTECTIVE FACTORS

Every homicide tells a story. Obituaries published by relatives and friends tell part of the story—the part that memorializes them. Descriptions of homicide cases by DVDR teams published in Annual Reports also only tell part of the story because they only know homicide victims as dead persons characterized by the presence of risk factors for lethality. Women who survived male partner attempts to kill them, and women with the same risk factors present who were not killed, were not included in the samples of women from whom information was collected by DVDR investigators, Consequently, their stories are not included among the stories told to DVDRs (Campbell et al., 1998; Cavanagh, 2003; Goodkind et al., 2004; Goodman et al., 2005). The result is that opportunities for making recommendations aimed at prevention grounded in knowledge of both protective factors and risk factors were lost.

Opportunities for making such recommendations can be restored by directing DVRDC investigators to ask questions about access to the individual and community protective factors described next.

Individual protective factors identified by some researchers include employment; stable housing; leaving a habitual coercive controlling intimate partner and not returning to reside with him; applying to family court for a relocation order in an undisclosed community; going into hiding; stop drinking; avoid arguing when one or both partners are or have been drinking; apply for a restraining/protection order and email a complaint to chief of police and the family court if it is not being enforced by police officers; maintain positive, supportive relationships with family and friends, especially those with whom you can share information and reside with if you are likely to experience imminent harm (Campbell et al., 1998; Cavanagh, 2003; Fleury et al., 2000; Goodkind et al., 2004; Goodman et al., 2005; Roehl & Guertin, 2000).

Community-based protective factors include access to subsidized housing, access to women's shelters, subsidized daycare, employment opportunities for women, access to financial resources, and residing in a community with high collective efficacy where neighbors and residents watch out for and help each other and intervene when protection from harm is warranted (Centers for Disease Control and Prevention, 2016). In short, any activity or community resource that promotes the economic and social independence of women is a protective factor for them (Dugan et al., 2003).

Two practice implications can be derived from the presence of protective factors in every story of femicide. One, DVDR investigators should be required to collect information on both risk and protective factors from samples of women that include (a) victims of femicide, and (b) victims of male partner violence and/or coercive controlling tactics during the past 12 months (Turner et al., 2019, p. 31). Two, questions about the use of protective factors should be included in the risk assessment instruments administered by police officers attending 911 calls, as well as staff in family violence prevention organizations and agencies.

SELECTION OF HOMICIDE CASES

DVDRs vary greatly with respect to the selection of homicide cases for review. The British Home Office identifies their impact on the community, as well as new criteria DHRs can use in selecting homicide cases to review. The Calgary, Alberta DVDRC reviews all domestic violence-related homicides but conducts in-depth reviews of homicides representing different age groups, and geographic locations (UNODC, 2023). The

Ontario DVDRC, the Santa Clara FRT, and the Ontario DVDRC state they review all domestic violence-related homicides that occur in their respective jurisdictions.

It is important to know how decisions about selecting which homicide cases to review are made by domestic violence homicide review advisory group members because it affects the generalizability of the findings they report on the impact of their recommendations. Findings reported by Boughton (2021, pp. 169–72) indicate that some homicide cases are not reviewed because the funds associated with the cost of including them were not available. Consequently, we do not know how recommendations based on a subset of cases in one year apply to adjudicated domestic violence-related homicide cases that were not reviewed in the same year. Researchers Cook et al. (2023, pp. 12–13) also raise questions about how the lack of information about decisions "not to undertake a DHR are made." The lack of clarity or transparency on which homicide cases are selected and why, raises several troubling questions. One of them is why adjudicated domestic violence-related homicide cases where police officers were convicted of murdering their intimate partners did not appear to be included in the Annual Reports reviewed by the author of this book. Of course, the possibility that no police officer perpetrated a domestic violence-related homicide in Santa Clara County since 1994, the Ontario DVDRC since 2003, or West Berkshire since 2011 cannot be ruled out.

SELECTION OF ADVISORY GROUP MEMBERS

For researchers Websdale, Sheeran, and Johnson (2001) members of DVDRs advisory teams, committees, and panels should include forensic pathologists, medical personnel with expertise in domestic violence, coroners and medical examiners, county health department staff who deal with domestic violence victims' health issues, representatives of local child abuse agencies that are involved with domestic violence abuse reporting. The Ontario DVDRC selects representatives with expertise in domestic violence from "academia, law enforcement, the criminal justice system, the civil justice system, the health-care sector, social services and other public safety agencies and organizations" (Ontario DVDRC, 2018, p. 3).

For the UNODC (2023, pp. 17–18) an ideal DHR Panel would be composed of individuals possessing complementary types of expertise, including:

- Knowledge of community-based responses to family violence and femicide;

- Credibility with community-based organizations and agencies and experience of working strategically with them;
- Represent organizations and agencies providing support and services to victims and perpetrators of family violence;
- Senior members of the organizations and agencies they represent;
- Theoretically informed about the dynamics underlying gender-based violence against women;
- Represent diverse communities.

The Domestic Violence Fatality Review National Summit (1999, p. 5) is unique in that it included "Survivors of domestic violence" in its list of "key members" of FRTs.

Many, if not most membership lists published by DVDRs elicit the following concern: they tend to exclude members representing co-victims, survivors of attempted femicides, and hospital emergency ward staff.

The inclusion of survivors of attempted male partner-perpetrated femicides and co-victims of femicide is warranted on the grounds of the quality of the contribution they can make to deliberations resulting in recommendations aimed at preventing femicide.

In 2021, 788 domestic homicides were reported by Canadian police forces (David & Jaffray, 2022). The number of co-victims of domestic homicides during 2021 was 1,220. This figure seriously underestimates the number of co-victims because it does not include close relatives residing in other households, and that 1,260,850 persons in Canada reside in five-person households (Globaldata.com) (Gross, 2007) projects an outcome in which there are between six and 10 family co-victims of femicide for one direct victim of domestic homicide in the United States.

Given "conflicting suggestions" included in the Fatality Review National Summit (1999, p. 13) co-victims of domestic homicides tend not to be selected to represent co-victims in advisory group deliberations. The absence of "survivor and co-victim voices" in advisory group deliberations is an ethical and substantive problem unacknowledged by FRT and DVDRC—but not DHR—review advisory group members (Domestic Violence Action Plan, 2012; Rubenstein, 2004). It is a problem of great substance because the voices of those who experienced attempted femicide by a male partner, as well as co-victims of femicides who knew a lot about the dead person as a living one, tend not to be heard during advisory group deliberations that produce recommendations aimed at preventing femicides (Boughton, 2021, pp. 241–44).

The inclusion of a senior hospital emergency ward physician or forensic nurse may also make a positive contribution toward achieving system change by increasing information sharing between hospital emergency wards and other healthcare and law enforcement agencies.

Findings reported by the UK Home Office (2016) reveal that hospitals were most frequently identified as the agency "where issues [problems] were identified with communication or information sharing between agencies" (p. 25).

The exclusion of co-victims and emergency ward physicians from DV-DRs stands in sharp contrast to the inclusion of representatives of police officers in all but one of the DVDRs (Ontario) reviewed by the author. The presence of police officers raises many concerns for a variety of reasons. One of the most prominent of these is that they represent police bureaucracies that "operate via a top-down hierarchal structure . . . and an organization ethos in opposition to DVDR advisory groups that present themselves as egalitarian multi-agency voluntary groups" (Boughton, 2021, chap. 7).

Other concerns are grounded in the belief that police members of DVDR advisory groups are experts in domestic violence (Ontario DV-DRC Annual Report, 2018, p. 1; Santa Clara County DVDRC Annual Report, 2013, p. 3), and that their expertise will be reflected in advisory group discussions and recommendations aimed at preventing family violence and femicide (Boughton, 2021, pp. 189–94).

Police officers serving as advisory DVDR group members do have expertise in enforcing laws against committing violent crimes against the person, but they do not necessarily have expertise in understanding the dynamics underlying male partner violence and femicide. Moreover, while police officers serving as DVDR advisory group members represent the majority of law-abiding, safety-promoting, helpful police officers, they also represent a very small minority who are complicit in the murder of their female partners and a larger number who physically and emotionally abuse and coercively control them.

Femicide Census researchers Long et al. (2020) found 13 of 16 of the women who were murdered by police officers were murdered by a current or former partner. Researchers Mennicke and Ropes (2016, p. 160) systematically reviewed the methods and estimates of physical violence and psychological abuse against females by their partners who were police officers. They found 21.2%—twice the national US average rate—perpetrated self-reported physical violence, and an average of close to 25% of them perpetrated "acts of psychological violence at some point in their careers." Estimates reported by researchers French and Fletcher (2023) reveal that police officers are "four times more likely to engage in domestic violence than the general (U.S.) population."

Police officer members of DVDR teams and committees share the values and norms of the police subculture. As advisory group members, these officers are likely to make or support advisory group recommendations on holding perpetrators of femicide accountable and culpable. On the other hand, as members of the police subculture, they may be less likely to support recommendations aimed at making police bureaucracies and police officers accountable for conduct resulting in the death or injury of intimate female partners (Boughton, 2021, pp. 189–93). Three practice implications can be derived from the evidence and argument presented here.

One, select female intimate partner survivors of attempted murder and co-victim family members as members of domestic violence homicide death reviews. Two, select doctors or forensic nurses staffing hospital emergency wards as advisory group members because their inclusion may well result in recommendations aimed at eliciting disclosure of male partners perpetrated life-threatening injury cases not only to the police but also to DVDRs.

Three, make recommendations to chiefs of police requiring the inclusion of mandatory police education and training courses on (a) risk factors such as stress, macho subculture, alcohol use/abuse, police union protection from discipline or prosecution for violence against intimate partners by police officers as risk factors for domestic violence by police officers, and (b) understanding the dynamics underlying the use of criminal violence and harassment against their intimate partners. Two, consider, excluding police officers from membership in DVDRCs, teams, and panels on the grounds of their probable opposition to recommendations that may hold police officers accountable by their police service employer.

CONTRADICTORY OBJECTIVE

One fundamental contradiction between the objectives of prediction and prevention is identified in this segment. In the Annual Reports published by DHR, risk factors are consistently referred to as predictors of femicide. For example, the finding that 67% of all cases reviewed by the Ontario DVDRC had seven or more risk factors is significant because many domestic homicides may have been predicted and prevented with earlier recognition and action aimed at identified risk factors for future lethality (Ontario DVDRC Annual Report, 2018, pp. 8–9). Consequently, DVDR advisory group members can legitimately be described as using a predictive model. Recommendations derived from a predictive model are grounded in the assumption that prevention depends upon knowing about risk factors for past femicides that predict the probability of future femicides.

At the same time, when multiple risk factors are also used by DVDR advisory groups to make recommendations aimed at organizations and agencies whose purposes include preventing family violence and femicide, they are also using a prevention model (2018 Report, p. 17, graph 2). In this model, risk factors are used to identify appropriate interventions by one or more community-based organizations to whom recommendations were made. However, increases in the ability to predict femicide based on the presence of multiple risk factors decrease the ability to prevent femicide because prevention will require information sharing, collaboration, and coordination of interventions by multiple organizations and agencies. The greater the number and variety of organizations and agencies to whom recommendations are made, the greater the difficulty of achieving coordinated, intra-agency and interagency responses to DVDR recommendations (Thornton, 2017, p. 39).

HIERARCHY OF VOICE

DVDRs present themselves as egalitarian, multi-agency groups where the voices of all advisory members are heard and are reflected in the recommendations made to community-based organizations and agencies. Researchers Boughton (2021) and Watt (2010) investigated the process of producing recommendations by observing DVDR deliberations, and/or interviewing advisory group members.

Boughton (2021, chap. 7) found "the problem of being a death review committee member is about hierarchy" because some sources of knowledge were found to be privileged and therefore dominant (Robinson et al., 2019, p. 16). Specifically, findings reported by these researchers indicate that greater weight is given to the voices of high-ranking, long-serving professionals than recently appointed advisory group representatives. Greater weight is also given to the voices of representatives of statutory organizations (e.g., law enforcement agencies, coroners or medical examiners), than the voices of those who represent nonstatutory (voluntary) organizations and agencies (e.g., agencies staffed by advocates for women).

With respect to the implementation of recommendations, the voices of advisory group members who occupy high-ranking positions in the organizations and agencies they represent are also likely to be given greater weight in DVDR deliberations because their position enables them to monitor and track recommendations, and consequently facilitate their implementation (UNDOC, 2023).

Boughton (2021, chap. 7) asked respondents questions about the distribution of power in DHR deliberations. Her questions elicited these responses: "in the DHR context the problem of being a panel member is about hierarchy"; "higher ranking panel members use the DHR process to pursue ulterior, organisation objectives"; "why certain individuals protect the organisations they represent are always at the DHR"; "DHRs are very police driven"; "one individual dominated discussions, talking over others regularly . . . another member made a suggestion but was ignored."

Some panel members she interviewed "recalled instances where certain individuals who were acting on their organisation's behalf, pushed certain agendas and attempted to control discussion points on their organisation's behalf." She also found "in all case studies, one or two panel members attempted to control discussion points" (Boughton, 2021, p. 185), and that interaction among representatives of different organizations and agencies was "not always harmonious and can induce arguments between agency panel members" (Boughton, 2021, chap. 5).

The practice implication that Boughton (2021) derives from her observations and interviews is "DHR specific training that "cultivates the confidence of advisory group members to challenge and be actively involved in DHR deliberations."Participation in Practitioner Training (Ancillary Resource) is one way of increasing the effectiveness of DVDR group deliberations.

Chairs of DVDRs vary greatly in their ability to facilitate equal opportunities for communication and collaboration among all advisory group representatives of organizations and agencies (Boughton, 2021, pp. 168–72). The egalitarian, collaborative, consensus-seeking model used by the Circle of Experts subcommittee of the Indigenous Advisory Committee (Government of Canada, 2022) may be worth emulating.

Alternatively, training in how to be an effective chair could be made a requirement for an appointment to chair a DVDR (Ancillary Resource). After all, if communication and collaboration among advisory group members cannot be achieved by advisory group members themselves, the prospect of achieving the same outcomes by organizations and agencies to whom recommendations are made may suffer.

PUBLIC AWARENESS

Increasing public awareness is an important stated purpose of many DVDRs. Reports to the media are the usual means used to achieve this end. A Google search for Annual Reports by DVDRs will reveal that few if any of them are published annually online. Moreover, segments of reports that members of the public may be interested in learning about, such as what to expect when a police officer responds to an emergency domestic violence call are not included in any of the reports that were reviewed by the author. The intermittent publication of Annual Reports and their poor quality—facts presented in them were stated, but not qualified or interpreted in terms of their meaning and underlying dynamics—was revealed by Cook et al. (2023, p. 6).

The practice implication derived from these findings is to publish Reports Annually and take suggestions made by Cook et al. (2023), into account in submitting reports to the media.

DILEMMAS

A dilemma refers to having to choose between two equally undesirable alternatives such as a rock and a hard place. The two noteworthy dilemmas described in this segment refer to dilemmas faced by female victims of male partner violence and by physicians working in emergency departments of hospitals. The first dilemma is described under the subheading of "Staying and Leaving." This is a dilemma because the choice between staying and leaving may be an equally hard alternative. The second dilemma is described under the subheading of "confidentiality and safety." This is a dilemma because physician disclosure of patient identity may decrease patient disclosure of the cause of their injuries and consequently hinder attempts made to decrease future attendance at the emergency department. Disclosure may also result in the administration of sanctions for violating legal, professional, and social norms governing the relationship between physicians and patients.

STAYING AND LEAVING

Women experiencing violence and the use of coercive control tactics by their male partners face the following dilemma: Stay and risk being killed, or leave and risk experiencing the same fate. Investigation of the Annual Reports of domestic violence homicide reviews will reveal no recommendations aimed at persuading victims of male partner violence and coercive control tactics to resolve this dilemma by staying or separating (Irving & Chi-Pun Liu, 2020; Kirkwood, 1993; Penfold, 2005; Vallee, 1998).

At the same time, statistics on separation as a risk factor sent to the media are likely to lead victims of male partner violence and criminal harassment who read them to conclude it is safer to stay and do what they can to avoid being repeatedly victimized. This choice is grounded in learning that "separation was a risk factor for femicide in 70% of the cases" reviewed by the Ontario DVDRC (2018) when leaving is really far safer than staying for the vast majority of mothers who decide to separate for good. Actually, a relatively small fraction of mothers—less than 1% (Chapter 8) in this book—were killed by the male partners they separated from. Of course, even one femicide is one too many, but the adverse consequences of unintentionally inflating the risk of femicide following separation should also be included in DVDR submissions to the media.

Also, DVDR advisory group members would be safe in assuming that many abused female mothers would prefer to stay with the fathers of their children but want the violence to stop (Goodmark, 2004).

Two implications for practice flow from the evidence and argument presented here. One, DVDR Annual Reports should also make recommendations aimed at promoting the safety of mothers who want to stay (Peled et al., 2000). Examples include participation in family mediation or other programs that teach couples how to settle conflicts by focusing on the underlying interests of the parents rather than the positions they take during arguments (Ellis et al., 2015; Fisher & Ury, 1972).

Two, the meaning of statistics included in DVDR Annual Reports and submitted to the media should be interpreted for readers rather than letting them speak for themselves (Rowlands, 2022).

CONFIDENTIALITY AND SAFETY

In Canada, physicians are legally required to disclose information under specified circumstances. The Canadian Medical Protection Association (CMPA) identifies eight circumstances where disclosure is mandatory. Unlike children in need of protection and elder abuse, abused women were not included as a named group requiring mandatory disclosure. However, they would be included if they were "shot, stabbed, or killed." Presumably, if they were strangled and would have died but for medical intervention in the emergency room, disclosure would not be mandatory but discretionary. If reporting strangulation attempts called for by three female Newfoundland police officers was made mandatory, it would solve the physicians' dilemma in favor of safety over confidentiality (Canadian Broadcasting Corporation, 2021; Glass et al., 2008).

Researchers Singhai et al. (2012) investigated "domestic violence and emergency room visits" in Ontario between 2012 and 2016. They found 10,395 (81.2%) of the visits were made by females. The female hospital visit rate per 100,000 was four times greater than the comparable male rate (25.5 versus 6.1). The source of information on these rates was not disclosed by ER physicians but the "ambulatory visits database" revealed one or more of the following: domestic violence, neglect, or abuse by a spouse, as well as other family and nonfamily members. To the extent to which mandatory disclosure is not required by ER physicians treating these patients, and patient confidentiality is emphasized by the CMPA, it is possible that none of them were disclosed to family violence prevention agencies. Consequently, it does not seem unreasonable to conclude that the physician's dilemma was solved by the choice of confidentiality over safety.

In the United States, laws governing disclosure by physicians vary across states. Some states have laws requiring the mandatory disclosure of visits for domestic violence-related injuries. One of the very few studies conducted on the association between visits to the ER by female victims of male partner violence and domestic violence-related femicides was published by Waldman and Muelleman (1999). These physician researchers studied 34 femicides, 15 of which were domestic violence related. Collectively, victims visited the ER 48 times, 20 of which were injury-related. Fourteen of the 15 women brought injuries with them to the ER on at least one visit.

The major finding reported by these researchers was that "nearly half of all women who were victims of a DV-related homicide had been in the ER within 2 years before their deaths." In addition to experiencing male partner violence serious enough to warrant a visit to the ER and possible hospitalization, victims may also disclose information about multiple adverse physical and mental health injuries inflicted upon them by the perpetrators whose violence—including nonfatal strangulation (NFS)—was the cause of their repeated visits to the ER (Glass et al., 2008). Multiple problems require a coordinated therapeutic response from family violence prevention agencies. Evidence indicating the ER physicians shared this information with these agencies was neither cited nor recommended by the two physician researchers. The evidence they did cite yields two conclusions. First, repeated ER visits by female intimate partner is a potent predictor of femicide. Second, the ER physicians' safety-confidentiality dilemma was settled by the choice of confidentiality over safety.

One practice implication flowing from the evidence and argument presented here is for DVDRs to collect information on the causes of visits to hospital ERs by victims of past femicides to decrease the probability and risk of future femicides in the same circumstances. Legislation may be required to obtain access to hospital ER data.

A second practice implication derived from findings reported by Glass et al. (2008) is for police officers, DVDR advisory group members, and ER physicians to increase their awareness of the "signs and symptoms of strangulation" included in the Strangulation Awareness Resource Portal (SARP) published online.

ACCOUNTABILITY

A review of over 800 DVDRC recommendations reveals that none of them hold the organizations and agencies to which recommendations were made accountable for not implementing them. The origins of the absence or lack of accountability can be traced to the adoption of the Federal Aviation Administration (FAA) investigation model in which "lessons learned" replaced "accountability and culpability" as the primary goal. This model was applied by the FAA in responding to concerns raised about the sequential crashes of the two Boeing 737 MAX crashes that resulted in the deaths of 346 six passengers and crew members.

These crashes were investigated by the Committee on Transportation and Infrastructure US House of Representatives in 2019.

A report on these investigations by a House of Representatives panel concluded that the crashes were caused by the "horrible culmination of failures by the plane-maker (Boeing) and FAA responsible for regulating airlines." An investigation of these crashes by Burridge (2020) led him to conclude that "Boeing's "culture of concealment . . . and an overly close relationship between Boeing and the FAA were partly to blame for them." An investigation of the 737 MAX crashes by CNN researchers yielded the same conclusion (Canadian National Network, 2023).

Subsequently, the FAA promised to "work with lawmakers" to implement improvements identified in the House panel report but did not promise to hold individuals and organizations accountable for egregious acts of omission and commissions that resulted in airplane crashes. The FAA promised to work with lawmakers to prevent future airplane crashes, but this promise was made only after it was held responsible and accountable for the two 737 MAX crashes.

Notwithstanding the findings reported here, "lessons learned" remains the sole or at least primary purpose, of the FAA. Among members of the public, and especially among co-victims of airplane crashes (friends and relatives), accountability for them was valued more highly than lessons learned.

In the Websdale et al. (1999, p. 2) publication, "preventive accountability" is identified as the blameless "lens through which domestic violence deaths can be reviewed." The use of this lens is evident in the Dallas FRT (2017, p. 3) approach that "seeks to provide accountability without assigning blame." One significant impediment to the use of this lens by DVDR advisory group reviewers is that DVDRs operate in the shadow of a no-blame subculture.

The DVDR no-blame subculture is one in which members of advisory groups are not held accountable for making recommendations, and the organizations and agencies to which recommendations are made are not held accountable for not implementing them.

The DVDR no-blame subculture is present in the context of a wider societal blame culture in which individuals and organizations are blamed and held accountable for violating legal and social norms/rules. Consequently, the behavior of domestic violence death review advisory group members is oriented/influenced by "no-blame" subculture in opposition to the wider societal "blame culture" where blameworthy individuals and organizations are blamed for violating social norms (Boughton, 2021, chap. 8; Tannen, 1998). One exception to the no-blame rule is that perpetrators of femicide are blamed by members of the wider society and DVDR advisory group members.

The downside of the no-blame subculture is that it eliminates accountability (responsible for not implementing recommendations), and culpability (punishment for not implementing them). The upside of this subculture is that it (a) encourages honesty and transparency during the process of deliberations leading to recommendations, (b) facilitates change, and (c) increases the motivation of organizations and agencies to reveal the steps they took, mistook, or did not take to implement recommendations and to communicate and collaborate with other relevant organizations and agencies. For example, a domestic violence professional interviewed by Boughton (2021, chap. 8) stated, "If you have a process that's trying to blame somebody for what's happened to somebody. . . . I don't think that you will get the appropriate recommendations for change."

Ideally, the no-blame subculture "can have a positive effect on discouraging organisational cover-ups of either innocent professional mistakes, or intentional malpractice." In practice, Boughton found "blame to be present within DHRs, albeit to varying degrees," and opposition to the no-blame culture on the grounds of "no-blame-no accountability." Thus, a police representative interviewed by Boughton stated, "it is important to highlight lessons learned . . . but to identify something to be learned from, you have to see that there's been a mistake made in the first place and if a mistake has been made, then there's someone responsible for that mistake" (Boughton, 2021, chap. 8).

One practice implication that can be derived from the findings reported here is for DVDRs to replace a no-blame subculture with a trust subculture where individuals and organizations are held accountable and culpable for egregious omissions and blame-worthy commissions (Dekker, 2009). To conclude that "investigating the relationships between service delivery systems has much in common with the approach used in safety and accountability audits" (National Domestic Violence Fatality Review Initiative FAQ, n.d., p. 3) is a step in this direction is not warranted because accountability is part of the subculture of safety assessments, but not part of the subculture of DVDRs.

EVALUATION

Accountability to taxpayers, foundations, and other organizations who fund them is one of the reasons for conducting independent outcome and process evaluations of DVDRs. Outcome evaluations assess the impact of DVDRs on the achievement of their stated purposes such as lessons learned, system change, and preventing family violence and femicide. Process evaluations focus on how DVDRs attempt to achieve these objectives. The product of independent evaluations of DVDRs is increased effectiveness in achieving its objectives to a point where the public health benefits of DVDR recommendations justify the expenditure of public funds by them. Major recommendations flowing from such an evaluation could include the mandatory implementation of DVDR recommendations promoting the safety of females whose male partners are assessed as being very likely to kill them, replacing a no-blame with a trust subculture.

The practice implication to conduct a process/outcome evaluation of state, provincial, and county DVDRs is warranted by the fact that they have not been independently evaluated since they were established more than 20 years ago.

INTERAGENCY COLLABORATION

The history of DVDRs described in Chapter 2 tells only a partial story of attempts made by communities to prevent family violence and femicide. The story is partial because it does not refer to the presence of another agency, Coordinated Community Response (CCR), with the same stated purposes of DVDRs that were established some years earlier. For example, the Duluth, Minnesota, CCR was established in 1980, about 14 years before the Santa Clara County FRT, and the first CCR in the United Kingdom was established about 10 years before the establishment of DHRs in the United Kingdom (Standing Together, 2021). In an the same online publication, its anonymous stated, "Whilst we are not part of the CCR it is essential they are following six recommendations drawing DHR and the CCR together" (p. 7).

After letting readers know that FRTs "in some form" exist in 45 states in the United States, authors of the National Domestic Violence Fatality Review Frequently Asked Questions publication (undated) indicate that FRTs in some jurisdictions "dovetail with, or naturally build upon the existing coordinated community responses to domestic violence" (p. 3). However, the jurisdictions are not identified and evidence supporting the assertion is not cited.

Currently, a DHR and a CCR are present in several communities in the United Kingdom. The London (England) borough of Haringey is one of them. Facilitating collaboration within and between statutory and non-statutory agencies is clearly the core function of both CCRs and DHRs. However, collaboration between CCRs on the one hand, and DHRs and FRTs on the other, does not appear to be a shared core function. The relationship between them appears to be more accurately described by the metaphor of a silo—in this case, two silos.

This conclusion is derived from the absence of any reference to CCRs in the history of DVDRs, or in Annual Reports published by DVDRs, the publications of Standing Together, creators of CCRs in the United Kingdom, and the creators of the CCR in Duluth, Minnesota. The conclusion applies to the absence of evidence demonstrating collaboration in practice rather than, or in addition to, words in print describing the relationship between CCRs and DVDRs.

One obvious practice implication derived from the evidence cited here is for advisory groups DVDRs and CCRs to share information and collaborate.

FEMICIDE-SUICIDE

The impact of murder-suicide on family members and the wider community has been described as "devastating" by researchers Brennan and Boyce (2013). These researchers underestimate the devastation caused by murder-suicide because the violent crime of homicide includes both murder and manslaughter, and the statistics they cite refer only to victims killed by married and common-law spouses accused of murder. Specifically, spouses accused of murder represent only 39.5% of the total number of spousal homicides (n=871) in Canada between 2000 and 2011 (Lindsay, 2014).

The homicide-suicides referred to here are misnamed because 95% of the perpetrators were current or former male partners. In the paragraphs that follow femicide has been substituted for homicide because femicide has not yet been included as a violent crime in the criminal codes of Canada, the United States, or the United Kingdom.

The findings presented here provide a compelling rationale for DVDRS to review homicide-suicides and make appropriate recommendations aimed at preventing them. At the same time, extant recommendations aimed at preventing them do not appear to be informed by research on the complexity of homicide-suicide generally, and specifically, on whether DVDR recommendations aimed at preventing homicides are appropriate for preventing suicides (Banks, et al., 2008).

Femicide-suicides occur less frequently than femicides or suicides. However, they represent a substantial minority, over one-third, of the homicide cases reviewed by the Ontario DVDRC, and 50% of the cases reviewed by the Santa Clara County FRT in 2016 and the New Mexico FRT (Banks et al., 2008). Researchers Bourget et al. (2000) investigated 388 deaths investigated by the Quebec Coroner's Office. Thirty-seven percent of them (n=145) were homicide-suicides. As DVDRs in Canada, FRTs in America, and DHRs in the United Kingdom review homicide but not suicide cases, their definition of homicide includes homicide-suicides.

A review of findings reported by some researchers (e.g., Bourget et al., 2000; Cooper & Eaves, 1996; Ellis et al., 2015; Liem & Nieuwbeerta, 2010; Zeppegno et al., 2019), found (a) suicides following homicides only occurred when a female and/or children were killed by a male partner, (b) that the probability that femicide-suicides are suicides cannot be ruled out, and (c) that homicide-suicides are a distinct phenomenon, different from femicides and suicides with respect to "event characteristics" or circumstances. The circumstances in which several femicide-suicides occur are described in DVDRC Annual Reports and are included here.

In the three Ontario DVDRC cases described here, homicides invariably precede suicides. Therefore, it would appear to be appropriate for DVDRs to define them as homicides and make recommendations appropriate for preventing homicides. Support for this conclusion is provided by a sample of four cases reviewed by the Ontario DVDRC.

Case 2016-09 *involved the homicide. Of a 25-year-old female by her 38-year-old common-law partner who subsequently committed suicide. The couple had been separated but reconciled about a week before the homicide-suicide.*

Case 2016-18 *involved the homicide of a 46-year-old woman by her 57-year-old husband, followed by his suicide. The perpetrator controlled most of the victim's daily activities and there was a history of violence within the family. Family dynamics were influenced by cultures, religion and language.*

Case 2018-18 *involved the homicide of a 62-year-old woman by her 64-year-old husband who subsequently died by suicide. The couple had been married for 40 years and was in the process of separating, The perpetrator had a valid firearms license.*

Case 2016-01 *involved the homicide of a 26-year-old woman by her 32-year-old former boyfriend who subsequently committed suicide. Both died of shotgun wounds. The perpetrator had a license for the possession and acquisition of a firearm, despite his criminal record and mental health history.*

The fact that homicide preceded suicide in these cases, as well as in all the other cases of homicide investigated by police officers and coroners or medical examiners, would lead DVDR advisory group members reviewing homicide-suicide cases from these sources to make recommendations aimed at preventing homicide rather than suicide, because homicides are always perpetrated before suicides, and never occur after a person commits suicide. Consequently, homicide can be a risk factor for suicide, but suicide cannot be a risk factor for homicide.

However, the possibility that suicide is, or can be, a risk factor for homicide-suicide is strongly suggested by findings reported by researchers who collectively investigated well over 600 homicide-suicides over the past 20 years. The findings reported by these researchers were based on different samples, study designs, theories, and methods of analysis (Bourget et al., 2000; Cooper & Eaves, 1996; Edouard-Notredame et al., 2018; Ellis et al., 2015; Liem, 2010; Liem & Nieuwbeerta, 2010; Marzuk et al., 1992; Polk, 1994; Regoeczi & Gilson, 2018).

A review of the findings reported by them revealed similarities in the presence of risk factors and triggering events for homicide, suicide, and homicide-suicide (e.g., history of physical violence, substance abuse, depression, jealousy, gender of perpetrator and victim), and triggering events (e.g., separated or separating, arguments). Risk factors for cases where spousal homicides were perpetrated by male partners who were motivated to commit suicide (suicide-homicides), but only immediately after they killed their female partners, were not clearly differentiated from cases where male partners who intended to kill their female partners and then kill themselves after thinking about doing it for some time, and then feeling unbearable remorse (homicide-suicides).

A timing rule does not appear to be used for differentiating femicide-suicide from suicide-femicide cases. The two cases described next illustrate how the application of such a rule can be used to differentiate femicide-suicide from suicide-femicide cases.

In the following Ontario case, Linda Batstone murdered her eight-year-old daughter on December 14, 2014, by suffocating her. She was found guilty and sentenced to serve 15 years in a federal penitentiary. Ten years later—January 4, 2024—she committed suicide while she was incarcerated. Evidence presented at her trial indicated that she intended to kill herself because she did not want to leave her daughter with the father from whom she was separated (Canadian Press, 2024).

If the definitions of Marzuk et al. (1992) and Li and Chen (2023) were applied to this case, it would be appropriately defined as a homicide rather than a homicide-suicide or suicide-homicide, because the act of suicide was not perpetrated within 24 hours following the femicide.

In the second case, one that "rattled the community" of North York in Ontario (Mosleh, 2024), the perpetrator Robert Graham, who was confined to a wheelchair following a car accident, stabbed his wife, Ulrike, to death with a knife, and then killed himself with the same knife. If the same time rule was applied to this case, it would be defined as a suicide-femicide because the suicide was perpetrated immediately after the femicide.

Findings reported by Banks et al. (2008) reveal that all but two of the 46 homicide-suicide cases reviewed by the New Mexico FRT were perpetrated within one day of each other. However, most if not all of them could have been "extended suicides" (Palermo, 1994; West, 1965). That is to say, they were preceded by depression and rage instigated by the perceived infidelity of the female partner or her decision to separate. As these factors were not measured by Banks et al. (2008), they cannot be used to challenge their definition of extended suicides, and the appropriateness of New Mexico FRT recommendations aimed at preventing them.

Finally, when prior suicide attempts are identified as a risk factor for femicide in DVDR Annual Reports (e.g., Annual Report 2019, p. 32), recommendations aimed at preventing suicide tend not to be made to community-based organizations and agencies specializing in suicide prevention. Two examples follow.

In the 2019 Annual DVDRC Report, homicide case 16 included "Prior suicide attempts by [the male] perpetrator" who killed his intimate female partner. Prior suicide attempts are a fairly reliable predictor of suicide-femicide, but this case was defined as a homicide. The DVDRC recommendation was not made to suicide prevention agencies but to the Ministry of Health and Long-Term Care in dealings in contacts it has with "cases arising from recent immigration" (p. 50). In the second "prior suicide attempts" to femicide case included in the 2019 Annual Report, a recommendation was not made to practitioners specializing in suicide prevention, but to "addiction counsellors and nurses," and "additional training in education on the issue of domestic violence."

DVDRs located in the office of the coroner or medical examiner review many domestic violence-related homicide cases involving homicide suicides and suicide-femicides. As coroners and medical examiners are the source of homicide cases reviewed by DVDRs in the United States and Canada, their definitions of homicide-suicides matter because only domestic violence-related homicides and homicide-suicides are reviewed by DVDRs. If coroners were also required to refer domestic violence-related suicides to DVDRCs, then the criteria identified below can be used to differentiate homicide-suicides from suicide-homicides, and recommendations prioritizing the prevention of homicides from recommendations prioritizing the prevention of femicides.

The presence of a perpetrator and a female victim at the death is one factor that differentiates homicide-suicides from suicide-homicides. When (a) this situational factor, (b) the risk factors of past attempts to commit suicide, depression and alcohol use/abuse and (c) the triggering events of separation or infidelity, actual or perceived, are co-present,

DVDR advisory group members are much more likely to be reviewing a case of suicide-homicide than homicide-suicide.

One practice implication derived from the evidence and argument presented here is for DVDRs to collect data on the presence or absence of the perpetrator and victim at the death scene, the time of death of the homicide, and the suicide from the office of the coroner or medical examiner, or the primary healthcare records of perpetrator and victim. The current practice of using the word "subsequently" or "afterward" in Annual Reports (the New Mexico FRT excepted) to refer to when the suicide following the homicide occurred is too vague to reliably differentiate homicide-suicides from suicide-homicides.

One significant result of determining if the homicide case being reviewed is a homicide-suicide or a suicide-homicide is that recommendations aimed at preventing homicides/femicides are appropriate for the first case, and recommendations aimed primarily at preventing suicide are appropriate for the second case. As domestic violence-related suicides "probably occur five, six or seven times" more frequently than domestic violence-related homicides (Moncton-Smith, 2021), they should also be referred to DVDRs for review. Given the relatively high rate at which homicide-suicides are reviewed by DVDRs—almost 40%—and the salience of depression as a precursor of suicide, a second practice implication is to include a forensic mental health professional as an advisory group member in DVDRs (Banks et al., 2008, p. 1075).

ARGUMENTS

Johnson and Hotton (2003, p. 80) investigated 846 females and 210 males who were victims of intimate partner homicides. They found that "The majority of homicides occurred within high conflictual situations." Arguments as a means of settling conflicts figure prominently in the description of homicide cases reviewed by the FRT, DVDRC, and DHR. However, recommendations grounded in an understanding of the dynamics underlying conflicts that are settled by femicides perpetrated by male intimate partners were not included in any of the DVDRs reviewed by the author. DVDR Annual Reports are replete with lost opportunities to link descriptions of homicide cases where arguments ended with murders perpetrated by male and female partners with an understanding of the dynamics underlying them.

For Lundy Bancroft (2002), a former of the EMERGE treatment program established in Massachusetts, underlying dynamics that can result in femicides originate in the male partner's "sense of entitlement" to the greater privileges of being a man compared with those associated with

being a woman as the primordial cause of a long list of coercive controlling tactics which, when they are resisted, cause "abusive arguments"
that end with femicides.

In the frequently cited dynamic described by Stets (1988), concrete
manifestations of a sense of entitlement such as a pattern of orders, demands, and expectations, are resisted or challenged by female partners.
Conflict settled by control-motivated violence restores control lost by resistance, but results in the loss of control in cases when he kills her. Stets
(1988) theory fills in spaces left by Stark and Hester (2018) who reported
findings indicating that femicide was strongly associated with coercive
control.

A major gap in the theories described here is that they do not explain
why most arguments instigated by controlling coercive male partners
do not result in femicides, but some do. Answers to this question are
provided by practitioners and researchers on conflict resolution such as
Gottman et al. (2002), Kirkwood (1993), Pruitt and Rubin (1986), and Winstock and Eisikovits (2008). Pruitt and Rubin (1986) describe the following
five stages of conflict resolution: violating a partner's sense of entitlement
or social or legal norms; proliferation of issues; generalizing from issues
to personal character attacks; threats; and obtaining support from allies.

Concepts interrelated in the dynamics identified by Gottman start
with a screen to determine the degree to which intimate partners bring a
relationship in which (a) "negative reciprocity is an absorbing state" and
(b) the amount of negative affect in nonconflict interaction, with them to
therapy sessions. Subsequently, fundamental attribution errors and the
persistent failure of attempts to repair conflicts tend to escalate the intensity of conflict to the point where the relationship may be ended by the
female partner. Successful repair attempts and de-escalating conflicts by
positive, instead of negative sentiment override, are keys to decreasing
the likelihood of separation, and consequently, postseparation nonfatal
and fatal violence.

The practice implication derived from the literature reviewed here is for
members of DVDR advisory groups to identify the dynamics underlying
the use of violence to settle arguments in all homicide cases where arguments were settled by homicide and make recommendations to agencies
offering programs promoting conflict de-escalation and the nonviolent
resolution of conflicts by intimate partners.

FIREARMS AND FEMICIDE

The statistics are compelling. Citing National Archive of Criminal Justice
Data (2015), Websdale et al. (2019, p. 3) report that "Fifty to sixty per cent

of male perpetrators of intimate partner femicide kill with firearms." Citing Violence Policy Center findings, they report that most femicide-suicides are perpetrated by male partners using firearms. An Everytown Research and Policy (2024, p. 1) research group report on gun safety cites findings indicating that male partners who abuse their female partners and possess firearms are five times more likely to kill them, than male partners who do not possess firearms. Findings from a multisite case-control study conducted in the United States replicate the Everytown findings. That is to say, researchers Campbell et al. (2003) also found female partners residing in a home in which firearms are present are five times more likely to be shot to death than female partners residing in a home where they were not present. In Canada, the Dixon Transition Society (2020, p. 2) reports findings indicating that access to a firearm "is the single greatest predictor that domestic violence will turn lethal." In Ontario, Canada, the Ontario Medical Students Association (2023, p. 2) found, "the presence of a gun in the home makes it 3.5 times more likely that a woman will die in a domestic violence incident than if a gun was not in the home." Firearms were used by male partner perpetrators of the femicide/homicides that led to the creation of the FRT in Santa Clara and the Ontario DVDRC, and also initiated the West Berkshire DHR review of the femicide perpetrated by Alan Pemberton against his wife, Julia, and the homicide of their son, William.

In the article referred to earlier, Websdale et al. (2019, p. 2) state DVDRs "provide a promising yet underutilized data source to understand the links between firearms and domestic related deaths." Findings supporting their DVDR under-utilization thesis follow. First, the "presence of a firearm in the home" is not included among the "Frequency of the fourteen common risk factors reviewed between 2003 and 2018" by the Ontario DVDRC. "Often or always has access to firearms" is included in the Santa Clara (2021, p. 20) FRT list of 17 "warning signs for victims" but is not included in "Warning signs for family members and friends." Second, "Does he or she have a gun or can he/she get one easily?" is included in the 11-item Lethality Assessment Screen police officers attending domestic disturbance calls administer to the person making the call, but specific Santa Clara FRT recommendations aimed at removing firearms from the home of the perpetrator by attending police officers who may have reasonable and probable grounds to believe a violent crime was perpetrated by a male against his female partner, are conspicuous by their absence. Third, a firearm was used to perpetrate femicide or femicide-suicide in 18 (35%) of 51 homicide cases reviewed between 1993 and 1997, but none of the six Santa Clara Death Review Committee recommendations (p. 15) referred to firearms. Fourth, in the 2018 Ontario DVDRC Annual Report, how the victims were killed was identified in only two cases that involved the use of firearms, and neither case elicited a recommendation to remove firearms from the home.

In sum, DVDRs may well do what Websdale et al. (2019), say they do—"include firearm use as part of their detailed analysis of intimate partner homicides" (p. 3)—but these analyses do not appear to result in recommendations aimed at removing firearms from homes where police officers responding to domestic violence calls have reasonable and probable grounds for believing a violent crime was committed, or likely to be committed in the near future.

The practice implication derived from the findings presented here is for DVDRs to recommend when police officers responding to domestic violence calls have reasonable and probable grounds believing a violent crime was committed by the perpetrator, they should confiscate firearms present in locations in the home identified by the victim during private interviews routinely held with them. Under this condition, firearms should be confiscated regardless of who owns them, and, if the parties reside in separate residences, regardless of in which residence the guns are present.

LESSONS LEARNED

Three lessons can be learned from reading this chapter. One, during the 20 or more years they have been operating, DVDR advisory groups do not appear to have perceived the need to implement many of the practice implications described in this chapter. Of course, it is possible that lessons were learned and implemented, but information about their implementation was not included in any of their Annual Reports. Two, defining homicide-suicides as homicides may have resulted in recommendations being aimed at homicide prevention that should have been aimed at suicide prevention. Three, the DVDRs reviewed in this chapter tend not to recommend the confiscation of firearms by police officers responding to domestic violence calls when they may have reasonable and probable grounds for believing a violent crime was perpetrated against an intimate partner.

6

✝

The Barriers Thesis

DEFINITION

In a paper published a few years ago, Musielak et al. (2020, p. 472) defined a barrier as "any circumstance, position or situational context that may increase an individual's vulnerability to violence." An assessment of this thesis is presented under the headings "Conceptual" and "Empirical."

CONCEPTUAL

The barriers thesis states that barriers are a risk factor for family violence and femicide in the sense that they are "circumstances that may make victims more susceptible to repeated incidents of violence by decreasing the victim's capacity to leave the relationship, seek assistance and increase her perceived helplessness" (Musielak et al., 2020, p. 472). This thesis elicits three concerns.

One, it commits its creators to an unacknowledged two-faced conception of barriers. One face directs attention to barriers as risk factors. The other face directs attention to overcoming barriers as a protective factor. In other words, a barrier can be a risk or protective factor depending upon whether it is overcome or not.

Two, the barrier clusters they refer to are gendered in that they are present only for female victims of male partner violence. Circumstances preventing or decreasing male perpetrator access to interventions provided by formal or informal helping agencies are either not regarded as barriers and/or are believed to make a negligible contribution to preventing family violence when they are overcome.

Three, as barriers include circumstances preventing the full disclosure of male partner violence to family violence prevention agency staff administering screening, and risk assessment instruments (p. 472), it is not unreasonable to expect the specific circumstances preventing full disclosure to be included in one of the four clusters they identify. This expectation was not met.

EMPIRICAL

Compelling evidence supporting the first part of the barriers thesis is provided by findings indicating that in arctic and subarctic indigenous communities in geographically isolated American and Canadian jurisdictions (Alaska, Yukon, Northwest Territories, and Nunavut) with the highest rates of family violence and femicide, are also ranked highest with respect to the presence of transportation, internet, land and water communication barriers preventing or decreasing access to police/legal, medical and other agencies providing supports and services to victims and perpetrators of male partner violence (Heidinger, 2022; Johnson et al., 2019).

In urban, rural, remote, and very remote communities any circumstance that makes it very difficult or impossible for a male perpetrator of intimate partner violence to be within physical reach of his former or current female partner is likely to be an effective barrier against future lethal or nonlethal violence against her. Examples of these perpetrator barriers include incarceration for life, court-sanctioned relocation in a nondisclosed distant community, and mother and children going underground (Goodmark, 2007). However, barriers preventing male perpetrators of family violence and femicide from accessing family violence prevention agencies are not included in the list of 20 dimensions of barriers listed by Musielak et al. (2020).

Findings reported in several Annual Reports indicate that a relatively high proportion of perpetrators and victims of intimate partner femicide overcame barriers to accessing community-based organizations and agencies. For example, the Hawaii domestic violence fatality review (Pobutsky et al., 2014) indicates in 95.6 of 45 homicides that were reviewed between 2000 and 2009, the perpetrator, victim, or both were involved with a variety of organizations and agencies providing support and services. Ninety-one percent of them were involved with healthcare providers, mental healthcare providers, local hospitals, and emergency medical services (Pobutsky et al., 2014, p. 85).

Findings published in the Florida FRT Report (2019, p. 19) reveal that almost half of the 27 victims contacted victim support services, a certified domestic violence center or the Department of Children and Family Services, and the same proportion of perpetrators attended a court-ordered batterer intervention program or contacted a faith-based organization or clergy. Between 2012 and 2016 the Dallas County FRT (2017, p. 5) reviewed 76 homicide cases. Over half (52%) of the victims and perpetrators contacted or were involved with a variety of organizations and agencies. Twenty-three (30%) of the 76 persons who were killed "sought police/legal interventions."

A review of Annual Reports published by FRTs in the United States indicates that a high proportion of female intimate partners who overcame barriers to accessing many of the barriers identified here were also victims of femicide. Does this mean women facing the highest risk of being killed by their intimate partners were (a) greatly over-represented among women who contacted community-based organizations and agencies, or (b) the agencies they contacted or were involved with did not communicate and collaborate or coordinate their interventions? Answers to these questions were not included in the article published by Musielak et al. (2020).

Findings reported for FRTs in the United States qualify the barriers thesis in that they indicate overcoming barriers to accessing some kinds of resources by victims of family violence increases the probability of family violence and femicide (Goodmark, 2004). The reader may recall that in all three femicide-suicide cases described in Chapter 2, contacting the police, applying for injunctions from the criminal court, or commencing adversarial separation or divorce proceedings in family court escalated the likelihood of femicide-suicide.

In addition to findings reported by practitioners, findings reported by Musielak et al. (2020), may not provide support for their own version of the barriers thesis. For example, they found barriers faced by femicide victims in their DVDRC sample (n=183) were located in the following four clusters: intuitive sense of fear, social isolation, mental health diagnosis, and low risk/barrier cluster.

The low risk of femicide/low barrier cluster is interesting because it includes the highest number of femicide victims and the lowest number of barrier dimensions. This finding contradicts the thesis that barriers are risk factors for femicide when those with the fewest barriers to overcome are overrepresented among femicide victims. Why did intimate female partners with the fewest barriers not contact family violence prevention agencies? In the absence of interview data on physically abused women who did not contact these agencies Musielak et al. (2020) cannot answer this question.

This gap was closed by Fugate et al. (2005). Unlike Musielak et al. (2020) who collected data on barriers faced by 183 female homicide victims included in Ontario DVDRC files, Fugate et al. (2005), interviewed the women in their sample. Findings reported by these researchers were based on the collection of data from a sample (n=491) of female partners who were screened in as victims of physical violence during the preceding 12 months but did not contact family violence prevention agencies. Specifically, Fugate et al. (2005), found 82%, 74%, 62%, and 29% of the women in the sample did not contact any agency or counselor, seek medical care, call the police and talk to family and friends respectively, "because the injury was not serious enough or talking to someone was not likely to be useful." These two reasons for not seeking help by overcoming barriers were reported for all four types of intervention identified by Fugate et al. (2005).

The four types of barriers—hassle, fear, confidentiality, and material loss—described by Fugate et al. (2005) were found to prevent or hinder access to all four sources of help identified by them. Specifically, physically abused women whose lives were difficult enough already, did not want the additional hassle of contacting an agency that might make help contingent upon them applying for a protection order, or leaving their abusive partners. They did not want to contact the police or press charges because of the hassle involved in becoming involved with agents of the criminal justice system, and the loss of control over the process of promoting their own safety following involvement with police and prosecutors.

Fear was found to be "a major deterrent to telling anyone—especially the police" because, unlike interventions aimed at promoting their own safety, police interventions aimed at the perpetrator may elicit a violent reaction to the aversive experience of the police coming to perpetrator's home, being arrested, charged with a violent crime, participating as a defendant in criminal justice proceedings and the possible loss of employment. Victim fear is included as a barrier by Musielak et al. (2020) and Fugate et al. (2005). However, fear of adverse consequences for breaching barriers is experienced by both perpetrators and victims in the Fugate et al. (2005), publication, and only experienced by victims in the Musielak et al. (2020) publication.

Furthermore, contacting the police or other formal agencies may result in specific material losses such as being deported if they are immigrants, "scooping" of their children by child protection agencies if they are mothers, evictions by landlords if they are renters, and the loss of family income if criminally abusive male partners are incarcerated. It is also relevant to note that for mothers who want to stay with their physically abusive partners but want the abuse to stop, contacting informal agencies providing support and services to abused women can be a barrier preventing them from obtaining these services when they make the pro-vision of services contingent upon leaving their abusive male partners (Sharp-Jeffs et al., 2018).

The barrier thesis also states there is a direct link between overcoming barriers to safety and feeling safe. This link may well depend upon the effectiveness of the treatments or interventions that are accessed. Find-ings presented in Table 6.1 by Goodkind et al. (2004) and Goodman et al. (2005), indicate that referrals to family justice services vary with respect to rates of re-victimization with the lowest self-reported rates being re-ported for "talking to a person in a domestic violence program" in the cross-sectional (29%) and longitudinal (21%) study. The highest rates of re-victimization—53% and 51% are reported for "participation in a substance abuse program"' in the cross-sectional and longitudinal study respectively. Re-victimization rates for shelter residents and participants in mental health programs vary greatly by study design—53% cross-sectional and 32% longitudinal for the former, and 53% and 35% for the latter.

In interpreting the findings presented in Table 6.1, it is relevant to note that differences in the effectiveness of the family justice system services referred to in Table 6.1 could be due in part to differences in the responses of perpetrator users of the service, and the agency staff administering the services. Findings reported by Robinson et al. (2019, pp. 5–10) indicate that recommendations made by domestic violence-related homicide advi-sory groups are not implemented effectively because users—often "toxic trio" persons with mental health, substance abuse, and physical violence problems—do not return to complete the program they started. In some cases, staff are "hoodwinked" by user-perpetrators into believing they were actually victims, or that the violent acts they were alleged to have perpetrated were actually just "marital relationship problems" all couples experience. In other cases, practitioners demonstrated "tunnel vision" grounded in a particular view of the person which narrowed the options being tried (Robinson et al., 2019).

The barriers to obtaining effective treatment experienced by users of family justice system services who may have had to overcome barriers to use them in the first place were not included in the clusters described by Fugate et al. (2005) and Musielak et al. (2020). Moreover, both groups of researchers share the unstated assumption that the barriers thesis need not be informed by the relationship context in which violence against female partners often occurs.

Findings based on the qualitative analysis of interview data from a sub-sample of 122 men and 136 women participants in the longitudinal (three-year) Violent Men Study conducted by Dobash et al. (2007) revealed that "violence takes place in the context of a relationship characterized by love

Table 6.1. Re-Victimization Rates Reported by Users of Family Justice Services

Studies	Talking with a person in a DV program ReV*		Reside in a shelter ReV		Substance abuse program ReV		Mental health program ReV		Contacted police ReV		Helped by a religious organization ReV	
Author/date	yes %	no %	yes %	no %	yes %	no %	yes %	no %	yes %	no %	yes %	no %
Goodkind et al. (2004)	29	71	53	47	53	47	53	47	42	58	42	58
Goodman et al. (2005)	21	79	32	63	51	49	35	65	25	75	46	54

*Re-victimized

Note: Cross-sectional, retrospective study design involving 160 nonrandomly selected women recruited from community-based agencies providing emergency services to domestic violence victims.
Longitudinal study design involving 406 nonrandomly selected battered women in a major city over three years.

and commitment and cannot be reduced to just the violence" (Cavanagh, 2003, p. 231; Kuennen, 2013; Towns & Adams, 2000). Love and commitment are also barriers that must be overcome multiple times when female victims of male partner violence decide to separate. In the sample studied by Cavanagh (2003, p. 241), 85% of the physically abused women separated and returned to live with their abusive partners several times.

IMPLICATIONS

Although there is some overlap in the barriers identified by Musielak et al. (2020) and Fugate et al. (2005), the implications "for service providers and communities" they draw from their findings are different. Four implications for practice are identified by Fugate et al. (2005). First, the need for increased awareness of the services and supports available to victims and perpetrators of family violence.

Second, services may be accessed without the requirement of separating from their abusive partners, obtaining a prevention order, being deported, or evicted. Third, ongoing evaluation of the degree to which the needs of victims are being met in a timely fashion by the agencies they contacted for help. Fourth, interventions by formal and informal agencies should not only prioritize victim safety but also respect the right of victims to self-determination (Fugate et al., 2005, p. 304).

The first two implications reported by Fugate et al. (2005) are reasonable and ought to be implemented by practitioners. Given the tendency of formal and informal agencies to prioritize the achievement of agency objectives (Storer et al., 2013), respecting the rights of victims to self-determination is likely to be contingent upon the degree to which they are not inconsistent with the achievement of agency objectives (Goodmark, 2004; Sharp-Jeffs et al., 2018, pp. 6–7).

The practice implication Musielak et al. (2020) draw from their findings is that helping agencies should take barriers into account when they attempt to promote the safety of victims by using screening, risk assessment, risk management, and safety planning instruments designed to promote the safety of victims. This practice implication suffers from evidence indicating that barriers are unlikely to be taken into account by helping agencies who did not even do risk assessments or did them poorly in 56% of the cases they responded to Monique (2019, p. 9). Long et al. (2017, p. 27) cite findings indicating that agency staff tend not to understand risk assessment, use risk assessment instruments inconsistently, and exhibit a narrow focus on physical violence. Moreover, Ellis, Stuckless, and Smith (2015, p. 175) found the absence of evidence indicating that risk assessment results in more effective risk management decisions.

DISCLOSURE

Finally, screening and risk assessment require disclosure of violence and coercive control tactics by male partners. Barriers to disclosing or experiencing these physically and psychologically harmful types of conduct to helping agency staff administer screening and risk assessment instruments have been published by some researchers (e.g., Heron & Eisma, 2021).

One important barrier is the reluctance of family violence prevention practitioners—especially healthcare professionals—to abandon face-to-face interviews as the method of administering screening instruments that yield relatively low rates of disclosure (Renker, 2008, p. 497). For example, Greenspun (2005, p. 17) cites evidence indicating that "17% to 30% of all women treated in hospital emergency wards are victims of domestic violence," but the use of a face-to-face screening instrument by staff at a hospital in Ontario yielded a disclosure rate of 4.8%. Compared with face-to-face screening, private computer self-administered screening strategies in healthcare settings "consistently identified a higher prevalence of IPV and were the approach preferred by most of the study participants in samples that varied in size from 144 to 2469" (Renker, 2008, p. 496).

Findings based on the analysis of six random controlled trials by Hussain et al. (2015, p. 60), found a computer-assisted, self-administered screen increased the odds of disclosing IPV by 37%, compared with a face-to-face administered screen, and by 23% compared with a self-administered written screen. Similar findings are reported by Ahmad et al. (2009) and Greenspun (2005).

Self-administered computer screens can facilitate the disclosure of barriers to accessing community-based resources experienced by victims of male partner violence and coercive control (Dugan et al., 2003).

However, creators of the most frequently DVDR recommended risk assessment instruments—The Lethality Assessment Screen (LAS), the Danger Assessment 2 (DA2), and the Domestic Abuse, Stalking, Harassment and Honour-Based Violence (DASH)—apparently did not find empirical evidence supporting the inclusion of "are you afraid of what your partner may do to you if you tried to obtain help from the police or other outsiders" as an item in their instruments. One reason for the lack of credible evidence may be that access to some resources (e.g., contacting the police or a divorce lawyer) may increase the probability of femicide, while entering a women's shelter, and second-stage housing in a location unknown to violent and coercively controlling male partners may decrease the probability of femicide. The potency of barriers as risk factors decreases significantly when some of them increase and others decrease, the probability of femicide.

Moreover, the inclusion of a "barriers" item/question in field-validated risk assessment instruments DVDRs recommend for use by police officers does not necessarily mean that it will actually be used by police officers responding the domestic violence calls. The use of DASH by police officers in the United Kingdom confirms the validity of this concern.

DASH includes 27 questions. The "yes, no, not known" answers to these questions administered by police officers attending domestic violence emergency calls are used to predict re-victimization of the same victim, and also locate the victim in high, medium, and standard classes of risk. Grading victims as high risk on the basis of a DASH score of 14 plus means they are at high risk of experiencing fatal or nonfatal but life-threatening injuries at any time in the future.

DASH, described by its creators as a field-tested "evidence-based tool that saves lives," was specifically designed for referring cases classified as high risk to MARAC (Multi-Agency Risk Assessment Conference). A MARAC is "a meeting where information is shared on the highest risk cases between representatives of local police, health, child protection, housing practitioners, independent Domestic Violence Advisors, probation and other specialists for statutory and voluntary sectors." Clearly, the use of DASH by police officers has significant implications for facilitating coordinated interventions aimed at promoting the safety of victims whose cases were referred to MARAC.

Researchers Turner et al. (2019) investigated the use of DASH by police officers who responded to 86,000 cases which they classified as high risk. They found police officers correctly classified 5.7% of the revictimized cases as "high" risk, and 94.3% of them as medium or standard risk, yielding a false negative rate (FNR) of 94.3%. This means almost 95% of the cases were misclassified. Consequently, cases that should have been referred to MARAC were referred elsewhere or nowhere. Also, 97% of the cases of high-risk or serious injuries cases were incorrectly classified as medium or standard risk, and police officer use of answers to DASH questions to predict future victimization was no better than tossing a coin (50%). With respect to predicting femicide, the FNR reported by Thornton (2017, p. 21) is 100%. That is to say, all five of the individuals who had prior contact with the police and subsequently murdered an intimate partner were not classified as high risk.

Selection bias and measurement error were cited as explanations for these dismal findings. Selection bias refers to the tendency of police officers to select and respond to some but not all of the 27 questions in DASH they are required to respond to in predicting re-victimization. Specifically, they tended to respond to the intensity of fear communicated by the victim, and whether or not the violence was getting worse. Answers to both of these questions were found to be poor predictors of re-victimization.

As the intensity of fear was not specifically related to fear about accessing barriers, it could refer to the fear of future male partner violence for several reasons—firearm in the home, past violence, ongoing coercive controlling behavior, safety of the children—unrelated to accessing barriers. Where the danger of experiencing fatal or serious nonfatal male partner violence is imminent, the victim may be transported to a women's shelter for reasons unrelated to the fear of accessing it. Moreover, if a question on barriers to accessing safety-promoting resources was included in DASH, police officers administering DASH may be ignored in assessing risk because different police officers ask and emphasize answers to different DASH questions.

Finally, disclosure alone will not accomplish the objective of promoting the safety of potential victims of femicide who reside in communities where (a) for any reason they cannot access protection and prevention resources available in them, and (b) resources are not available in the communities in which they reside.

LESSONS LEARNED

DVDR advisory group members can learn at least four lessons from the findings presented here. One, overcoming barriers to accessing family prevention services may be less effective in decreasing revictimization by disclosing barriers to practitioners, than the effectiveness of the services that are accessed. Second, accessing some barriers will help promote the safety and liberation of female intimate partners experiencing a pattern of male partner violence and coercively control, accessing—or attempting to access—other barriers may increase the probability of femicide. Third, disclosing barriers to police officers and community-based agencies providing support and services to women experiencing male partner violence may be one of the most important first steps victims can take toward promoting their own safety.

7

✛

DVDRC and Indigenous Peoples

During the past 500 years European settlers used "violence and narratives" to transform the vast land mass called Turtle Island by indigenous peoples into what is now known as North America. Settlers using the same means transformed the northern part of Turtle Island called Kanata (Iroquoian word for settlement) into Canada (Barker, 2022). The settler colonizer transformation of Turtle Island and Kanata is ongoing but not completely successful because Barker found spaces where colonial logic does not overwhelmingly structure social space. If new social spaces can be expanded, "new practical possibilities for decolonial action can be developed" (Barker, 2022, p. 3). The establishment of a DVDRC in Nunavut is conceived of as one practical possibility for decolonial action.

The contemporary context in which this chapter is being written is one in which the possibility of decolonial action through the establishment of DVDRCs in indigenous communities is diminished by the following findings. One is the absence of an indigenous person on the 15-person planning committee at the Fatality Review National Summit (McHardy & Hofford, 1999). Two is the absence of any reference to indigenous communities in publications that facilitated the creation of DVDRs in non-indigenous communities (Websdale, 2003, 2020; Websdale et al., 1999). Three, recommendations made by DVDRs located in indigenous communities are suggested for implementation in non-indigenous communities (Heidinger, 2022; Rosay, 2016).

Websdale (2020, p. 3) states that domestic homicide reviews (DHRs) were created in "modern [non-indigenous] functioning democracies" because they represent "a form of local democracy and civic engagement." Indigenous communities are not referred to in this article, but a reader is left with the unintended impression that DHRs are absent from indigenous communities because of the absence of local democracy and civic engagement in them. The possibility that these attributes were present in indigenous communities long before the arrival of settler colonizers to North America is well documented (Elson & Carmichael, 2022; Government of Canada, 2021; Holmes & Hunt, 2017). Acknowledgment of this historical evidence may help explain the positive contribution made by Websdale (2009) to the establishment of an FRT in an indigenous community in Montana.

Preventing femicide is one of the stated objectives of DVDRCs created in southern cities in Canada. However, the strategy of promoting the safety of indigenous women in remote northern Canadian communities on the basis of recommendations derived from the discovery of risk factors in southern non-indigenous communities diverts attention from the investigation of risk factors present in indigenous communities but not in non-indigenous communities (Holmes & Hunt, 2017, p. 1; Statistics Canada, 2018). Risk factors for family violence and femicide unique to remote northern communities in Canada are identified by Johnson et al. (2019) but they do not explain why violence is the major determinant of health in remote northern indigenous communities but not southern or remote non-indigenous communities.

This gap is filled by Paradies (2016), and researchers at the National Collaboration Centre for Aboriginal Health who found settler colonization to be the determinant of higher rates of family violence and femicide in indigenous communities, and self-determination to be a precondition for the creation and operation of safety-promoting agencies by indigenous peoples in their own indigenous communities (Holmes & Hunt, 2017, p. 1). Building upon findings reported by Holmes and Hunt (2016), this chapter is written with the following two objectives in mind. The first is to locate the roots of family violence and femicide in settler colonization. The second is to present evidence and argument supporting the creation and operation of a DVDRC in the subarctic/arctic First Nation of Nunavut.

Essential conditions for achieving these objectives are presented under three sub-headings. First, a definition that includes diverse indigenous communities is presented under the heading, "Nomenclature." Second, changes in the circumstances under which indigenous peoples lived prior to and following settler colonization are described under "Findings: Historical and Contemporary Indigenous Communities."

Third, under the heading "Settler Colonization Theory," settler colonization is used to explain why violence was not a major determinant of the health of people in indigenous communities before settler colonization but became one after settler colonization. Problems and prospects of establishing a DVDRC in Nunavut are discussed in the final pages of the chapter.

NOMENCLATURE

Canada's indigenous population includes three culturally diverse peoples: First Nations, Metis, and Inuit. In the Canadian Constitution and the Indian Act these peoples are defined as Indians and Aboriginals, respectively. In this chapter, Indians and Aboriginals are referred to as indigenous peoples for two reasons. First, because of their spiritual and economic link to the land and resources on which their traditional lifestyles were based long before the arrival of settlers from Britain and France (Saint-Germain, 2022). Second, their lands and resources were coveted by white Christian settlers who intended to stay and replace indigenous peoples on their own lands.

FINDINGS: HISTORICAL AND CONTEMPORARY INDIGENOUS COMMUNITIES

The Royal Commission on Aboriginal Peoples (1996) describes four overlapping phases in the history of relations between settlers and Indigenous peoples in Canada. The four phases are separate worlds, contact and cooperation, displacement and assimilation, and negotiation and renewal. Perusal of the content of these phases yields the conclusion that whether what's past is a prologue in the history of Canada and depends upon which earlier phase is being referred to.

Evidence cited by the Truth and Reconciliation Commission indicates that phase one where indigenous and white peoples lived in separate worlds created by the Atlantic Ocean is prologue to the separate worlds (reserves and majority group communities) created by settler colonists, the federal government, and their religious supporters. Phase two, where "furs were traded for tools and weapons, military help was provided by Indigenous people, intermarriage and mutual cultural adaptations" (Elson & Carmichael, 2022, p. 10), is prologue to Negotiation and Renewal in phase four. Phase three, displacement and assimilation, is a prologue to the creation of circumstances in contemporary indigenous communities where "violence remains a major determinant of health."

Canadian history can also be divided into the time prior to the War of 1812 between the United States, and its indigenous allies, and Canada and its indigenous allies, and the time after the War Canada won that "laid the foundation for British North America."

The time before the war (phase two) is described in these terms: indigenous nations were geographically isolated, able to dictate terms of engagement, left alone, or were able to reconcile their traditional teachings and ceremonies with some settler practices. "Ceremonies such as the Sundance and Potlatches, are rich and elaborate occasions that blend communal, spiritual and governance practices and protocols. Relationships and reciprocity with both humans and other-than-humans are common and reflect a holistic view of the world and the subservient nature of humans in it" (Elson & Carmichael, 2022, p. 9).

Findings reported for the precolonial and early settler colonial period before 1850, reveal that conflicts were settled peacefully by Elders, women, and kin; indigenous parents participating in egalitarian; and matriarchal families performed complementary gendered social roles. Indigenous women occupied positions of power and authority as peacemakers, healers, diplomats, translators, fur trade facilitators, mediators, and wives of British settlers (Kopp & Mannitz, 2022; Tait, 2007). Indigenous culture—language, beliefs, values, norms proscribing violence against women and children, and commitment to a way of life connected to the land—was inculcated in children by parents, as well as relatives, friends, and neighbors residing in different households. Van Kirk (1984) concluded that "socially, economically and politically, indigenous women were at the heart of both pre-colonial and early colonial societies and massively important for the survival of the first British settlers" (p. 4).

Under the precolonial conditions described here—egalitarian matriarchal families; women occupying position of power and authority in their communities; multiple persons involved in the socialization of children, and an ancestral and spiritual connection to the land from which they earned a living by fishing, hunting, trapping, and farming—family violence generally and femicide in particular did not appear to be a noteworthy phenomenon in pre- and early settler colonial indigenous communities (Baskin, 2006; Bopp et al., 2003; Holmes & Hunt, 2017).

Findings reported by Statistica Canada (2022) reveal that family violence and femicide became a significant health problem in post-settler colonization indigenous communities. For example, when Canada's 10 provinces and three territories are ranked in order with respect to the percent of their indigenous populations, they can be almost perfectly ranked in order with respect to the percentage of female homicide victims recorded in them, ranging from (86.7% indigenous population/100% victims) in Nunavut; to (under 2% indigenous population/2% victims) recorded for

Nova Scotia, New Brunswick, and Prince Edward Island. Three northern territories—Nunavut, Yukon, and Northwest Territories—and two western Canadian provinces—Saskatchewan and Manitoba—with the highest percentage indigenous populations also recorded the highest percentages of female homicide victims (Statistica Canada, 2022).

Attempted murders—murders that would have occurred but for emergency medical intervention—are not included in the rates of homicide or femicide reported here. If they were included, the completed attempted murder rate would double (Statistics Canada, 2019).

The indigenous population of Canada is distributed across 630 First Nations communities, representing 5% of the population of Canada (35.5) million). Over 11 years (2011–2021), indigenous women and girls accounted for 21% of all gender-related homicides (Statistics Canada, 2022). Compared with the rate of gender-related rate of homicides for all women and girls (0.54 per 100,000), the gender-related homicide rate for indigenous women and girls was three times higher (1.72) (Sutton, 2023, p. 24). During the same 11-year period, almost two-thirds (63%) of the gender-related homicides involving indigenous women and girls as victims were perpetrated by male intimate partners (Sutton, 2023, pp. 24–25).

In a 2015 Statistics Canada publication, the rate of homicide in indigenous communities was found to be significantly higher than the rate for people residing in non-indigenous communities. Findings reported in *The Daily* (2022) show that 44% of indigenous women experienced physical or sexual violence by a male intimate partner during their lifetimes. The comparable figure for non-indigenous women is 25%. Comparable figures for First Nations and Metis are 43% and 48% respectively (The Daily, 2022).

Findings from the Canadian General Social Survey (2014) reveal that indigenous female victims of spousal violence were over twice as likely (53% versus 25%) to fear for their lives than non-indigenous female victims. They were also more than three times more likely than non-indigenous women to experience postseparation intimate partner violence (22% versus 7%) (Just Facts, 2023). As a result of male partner violence, separation, and divorce, 38% of indigenous families are lone-parent families. The comparable figure for non-indigenous families is 21% (Indigenous Services Canada, 2020). Almost 8% (7.7%) of children from lone- and multiple-parent Canadian families are in foster care, but almost 53.8% of the children in foster care in Canada are indigenous (Statistics Canada, 2016).

Many, First Nations children do not grow up to become adults aged 25 plus because they commit suicide. Compared with non-indigenous youth aged 15–24, suicide rates for First Nations youth in the same age group are "five or six times higher" (Canadian Institute of Health, 2022). Rates of suicide among First Nations people (24.3 per 100,000 person-years at risk) are three times higher than the rate among non-indigenous people (8.0 per 100,000) (Statistics Canada, 2019).

Finally, findings included in the Report of the Royal Commission on Aboriginal Peoples (1996) reveal the significant over-representation of (The Daily, 2023). Findings reported by the Canadian Centre for Justice Statistics (2006) indicate the overall incarceration rate for Aboriginal people is nine times higher than the rate for non-Aboriginal people (117 versus 1,024 per 100,000). Aboriginal people represent 2.7 % of the Canadian population but account for 18.5 of the federal prison population.

In a 7-0 judgment, the Supreme Court of Canada (1999), noted that a male treaty Indian was 25 times more likely to be incarcerated in a provincial jail than a non-native, and a female treaty Indian was 131 times as likely. This court also identified "poverty, substance abuse and lack of educational and employment opportunities" as "aboriginal reserve circumstances" responsible for the very high rates of incarceration reported here. In the segment that follows settler colonialism is identified as the root cause of the "aboriginal reserve circumstances" described here.

SETTLER COLONIZATION THEORY

Settler colonization refers to a global type of colonialism "that functions—and continues to function—through the replacement of indigenous populations with an invasive settler society . . . and subject's indigenous peoples to forced assimilation and cultural genocide" (Global Social Theory, 2016; Bosch, 2017. Unlike the Normans who were gradually absorbed into Anglo-Saxon society via intermarriage after conquering England militarily in 1066, settler-colonists in Canada and the United States oppressed, segregated, and forcefully assimilated indigenous peoples as part of the plan to replace them on their traditional lands (Orange, 2024; Wolfe, 2006, p. 388).

Intersection theory states that people invariably occupy multiple statuses (old, disabled, and poor), and they can be oppressed on all or some of them. Settlers oppressed all indigenous men who simultaneously occupied the status of Indian, savage, or ignorant, and women who—in the eyes of settlers—occupied the status of Indian, immoral, or squaws.

The most frequently cited starting point for the historically layered and interconnected set of resources used by settler colonists and the Canadian state to achieve their economic, cultural, structural, and economic objectives, was "The Indian Problem." For Indian Affairs Agent and federal government politician Duncan Campbell Scott, the roots of the Indian Problem in Canada were "uncivilized and immoral" traditional lifestyles incompatible with a modern, white person-dominated capitalist society lifestyle.

In addition to committing the culturally biased fundamental attribution error of attributing indigenous lifestyles to the essential nature of indigenous peoples, rather than the circumstances under which they were forced to live (Miller, 1994), Scott's allegation simultaneously dehumanized Indian peoples and justified his proposed solution to "absorb (assimilate) them into the body politic" until there was no longer an Indian Problem in Canada (Rheault, 2011, p. 3). Evidently, Scott's solution to the Indian Problem in Canada was genocide with "exploitation of Indigenous peoples as a 'value add on' that varies in its duration" (Paradies, 2016, p. 84).

In the United States, the 1880 Congress supported the violation of treaties by prospectors and miners searching for precious metals by stating "An idle and thriftless race of savages cannot be permitted to stand guard at the treasure vaults of the nation which hold our gold and silver . . . . The Miner and prospector may enter and by enriching himself enrich the nation and bless the world by the results of his toil" (Websdale, 2019). This statement is consistent with Paradies's (2016) definition of franchise colonialism that "seeks to extract value from subjugated [American Indians] through exploitation, with extermination a mere side-effect" (p. 840).

One of the first genocidal steps taken by the Canadian government was the Indian Act (1876). This act rejected self-identity in favor of an agency of the Canadian government deciding who was and was not an "indigenous person" (Coates, 2008, p. 4). The Indian Act also facilitated cultural genocide by isolating First Nations peoples from contact with white settlers by segregating them on reserves, mandating the creation and control over Band Councils in over 600 contemporary indigenous reserves, and creating residential schools (Kopp & Mannitz, 2022, p. 8).

Nagy and Sehdev (2023) refers to residential schools as "the story of colonization" in which they were connected with Numbered Treaties and The Indian Act to enforce attendance in residential schools for indigenous children aged between seven and 15. The horrible conditions imposed on the children are described in detail by the Truth and Reconciliation Commission of Canada. In addition to emotional pain and feelings of despair at being separated from their families and communities, indigenous children attending residential schools were treated cruelly by their teachers—white religious missionaries. Survivors recall being "beaten and strapped . . . shackled to their beds . . . needles shoved in their tongues for speaking their native languages" (Truth and Reconciliation Commission of Canada, 2016, Vols. 1 & 2).

Harsh discipline and abuse were used by missionary teachers to inculcate English as the only language, and replace indigenous culture with British values, norms, beliefs, ways of thinking, feeling, and interacting (Truth and Reconciliation Commission of Canada, 2016, Vol. 2). When indigenous girls attending residential schools became mothers, mental illness (such as posttraumatic syndrome), alcohol and drug use, and poverty associated with difficulties in obtaining and keeping gainful employment, resulted in higher rates of child abuse, neglect, and the placement of their children in foster homes, than indigenous mothers who did not attend residential schools or non-indigenous mothers. Between 1951 and 1982, "scooping" indigenous children from their indigenous homes and placing them in the homes of non-indigenous parents represented a continuation of cultural genocide in another time and context (Johnson, 1983).

Before 1763, indigenous communities were impoverished economically by the loss of their lands and resources claimed by the British under the Doctrine of Discovery and Tullius Nullius. This doctrine gave British settlers the right to claim land that was perceived by them to be "uninhabited or unoccupied." After the Royal Proclamation of 1763, British settlers could claim land from its Aboriginal owners or occupiers, but only after it was sold to settlers by the British Crown, who created or helped create the proclamation in the first place.

Eleven Numbered Treaties were used by the Crown to acquire and sell ancestral indigenous lands to British settlers. During treaty negotiations, representatives of the government made written statements and oral promises about the terms of the agreements reached—special rights to specified treaty lands, regular cash payments to generations of indigenous peoples occupying these lands, right of access to hunting, fishing, and trapping grounds—that were deliberately excluded from the written agreements which carried far less weight for indigenous peoples than the verbal promises made to them by government negotiators (Albers, 2017; Filice, 2016; Starblanket, 2019). The impoverishment of indigenous communities was one outcome of the loss of their ancestral indigenous lands in exchange for verbal promises that were not kept. Even when the provisions (promises) were written, "the federal government demonstrated little interest in implementing them" (Kopp & Mannitz, 2022; Truth and Reconciliation Commission of Canada, 2016, p. 11).

In addition to creating gender inequality favoring males in the family by supplanting the indigenous, egalitarian multi-caregiver matriarchal family with the inegalitarian, nuclear, patriarchal, male-dominant British family form, male partner violence, and male dominance in indigenous communities was facilitated by exposure to models of powerful non-indigenous men—British settlers, agents of the Canadian state (Indian

Agents and the Royal Canadian Mounted Police)—and male federal government legislators who provided indigenous men with models of men who used their greater military and economic resources and coercive controlling tactics to achieve their economic, cultural, political, and spiritual objectives.

A review of the literature cited here supports the conclusion that settler colonization or state policies and practices are the root cause of the emergence and maintenance of contemporary indigenous communities in which intergenerational and multigenerational trauma experienced by indigenous people is associated with several adverse health-related issues: mental health problems, alcohol and drug use, poverty, and family disruption. In these communities, violent crime generally, "lateral violence" among indigenous family members, and male partner beatings and killings of female intimate partners, has been internalized and normalized (Brant, 2020; Campbell, 2007; Holmes & Hunt, 2017; Sutton, 2023).

The ongoing impact of settler colonization in Nunavut is captured in the following findings. First, in 2018 the highest number of homicides was reported for Nunavut since it was created in 1999 (Statistics Canada, 2018). Second, rates of family and nonfamily violence against women in Nunavut in 2019 were the highest in Canada. Specifically, they were 13 times higher than the rate for Canada (2,356 versus 183 per 100,000) (Conroy, 2021, Table 1.4). At the same time, Nunavut does not have a multi-agency voluntary body that facilitates collaboration between, and a coordinated response to family violence and femicide prevention by social service agencies, women's shelters, health care centers, Royal Canadian Mounted Police detachments, and family violence programs. A DVDRC in Nunavut would close this gap.

APPLICATION

The gap referred to here can be closed in one of two ways. One is by establishing the non-indigenous DVDRC model located in major cities in southern Canada. This model tends to ignore "the legacy of historical trauma as a result of the larger historical, social and structural context" (UNDOC, 2023, p. 41). It is interesting and relevant to note that settler colonization figures prominently in this context but was not theorized by 29 experts from 18 different countries who made an otherwise valuable contribution to the UNDOC publication.

The second one is to establish a blended model informed by knowledge of (a) indigenous settler colonization theory, (b) more general systems and patriarchy theories, and (c) story-telling as the primary method of collecting information on risk and protective factors for past femicides. Differences between the blended-indigenous and non-indigenous DVDRC models are revealed by comparing the models described in Figures 7.1 and 7.2.

Figure 7.1 describes a DVDR in which information from past homicide cases reveals risk factors for femicide and gaps in the system response to it. This information is collectively discussed by FRT and DVDRC advisory groups (teams and committees) in homicide reviews that include homicides, homicide-suicides, and suicides-homicides. These reviews produce nonmandatory recommendations to law enforcement, as well as to other community-based family violence prevention organizations and agencies.

In 2018, the DVDRC of the OCC for Ontario located in Toronto identified 15 risk factors for family violence and femicide in Nunavut. Recommendations aimed at preventing these adverse health outcomes were to be made to appropriate community-based organizations and agencies in Nunavut. The impact of any recommendations that were made on decreasing the prevalence of family violence and femicide in Nunavut remains unknown five years later.

One reason for believing they had no discernible impact is that none of the DVDRC recommendations were derived from an understanding of intergenerational and multigenerational trauma resulting from (a) attendance in residential schools or (b) the coerced/duplicitous relocation of Inuit families from homes in which they had lived traditional lifestyles for generations, to High Arctic locations where they lived under the following circumstances: "far away from families and long-inhabited communities . . . where they found little food, 24-hour darkness in winter and an un-familiar life that contributed to depression and alcoholism" (Campbell, 2007, p. 72; Onishi, 2023; Truth and Reconciliation Commission of Canada, 2016, p. 72).

Researcher Brownridge (2008) published a study aimed at "understanding the elevated risk of partner violence against aboriginal women." The findings he reported led him to conclude that "the elevated risk for aboriginal women is not due to any single risk factor, but rather a constellation of variables that may be linked to the larger experience of colonization" (Brownridge, 2008, p. 366). Johnson et al. (2019) identified seven risk factors for remote indigenous communities such as Nunavut. None of them are included among the 41 risk factors for femicide published in the 2018 Ontario DVDRC Annual Report.

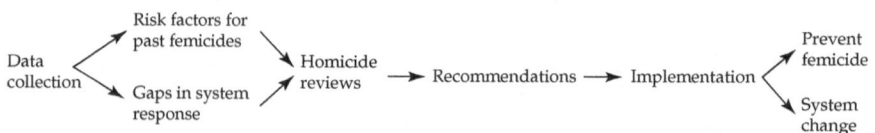

Figure 7.1   Non-Indigenous domestic violence death reviews operation. By author.

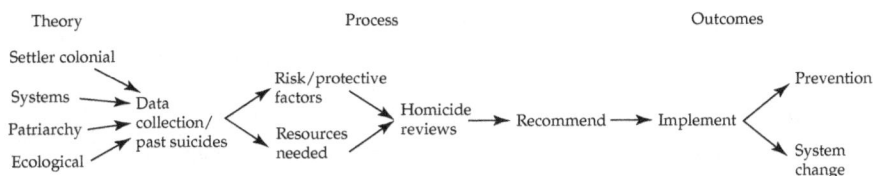

Figure 7.2. Blended Indigenous model of domestic violence death review operation. By author.

A letter written by the author and published in the Nunavut newspaper (*Nunatsiaq News*, July 17) advocated the establishment of a DVDRC in Nunavut. The DVDRC the author had in mind is described in Figure 7.2. Nine years earlier the Northern Territory Council of Social Services (Morton, 2014) identified five Focus Areas. Prevention was the first one. Recommendation 4: Establishment of an effective Domestic Violence Death Review process across the Northern Territory (NT) was included under the Focus on Prevention. The rationale for the creation of an NT DVDRC was conceived of as aligning "with strategy 5.2 of the National Plan to reduce Violence Against Women and their children." The establishment of a DVDRC in Nunavut (NDVDRC) is fully consistent with this National Plan.

Figure 7.2 describes a blended indigenous DVDRC. The starting point of the blended model is data collection on (a) risk and protective factors for past femicides told in stories by survivors of attempted murder and family members and (b) needed resources. Data collection is informed by settler colonization, systems, patriarchy, and ecological theory. The process begins with reviews of homicide, homicide-suicide, and suicide-homicide case reviews. Deliberations by DRVRC advisory group members yield recommendations made to appropriate family violence organizations, professionals, and practitioners. Recommendations informed by theory yield nonmandatory recommendations. Implemented recommendations result in system change and family violence/femicide prevention.

Four differences between the blended and non-indigenous models are noteworthy. One, the absence of theory in the non-indigenous model means that recommendations aimed at preventing family violence and femicides cannot be derived from an understanding of their root causes. Two, collecting information on both risk and protective factors for past femicides is likely to yield more reliable predictions for future femicides than collecting data only on risk factors. Three, collecting information from stories told by survivors of attempted femicide, relatives, friends, and neighbors of victims is more likely to reveal the patterning and dynamics underlying femicide than interviewing them or using instruments such as the DHR.

Four, unlike the non-indigenous model described in Figure 7.1, the blended indigenous DVDR is grounded in acknowledgment of the "entangled sovereignties" of First Nations peoples and the settler colonial state of Canada. The entanglements referred to here are the "creative tactics, calculated disruptions and negotiated compromises" used by both parties to maintain or extend control over land and access to resources made available by controlling land (Dennison, 2017).

Findings reported by researcher Dennison, suggest that the mutual use of "negotiation, concession and compromise" by the settler state and First Nations peoples "will lead to further entanglements," just as it did between the settler state of America and the Osage Nation in Oklahoma. Entanglements identified by Dennison are vividly described in *Killers of the Flower Moon*, a book published by Grann (2017) and made into a movie by Martin Scorsese.

A contemporary entanglement between the Biigtigong Nishnaabeg First Nation (BNFN) and the federal and provincial governments is provided by Dempsey (2023). The traditional land of the BNFN covers an area the size of Greece and lies adjacent to Lake Superior in Northern Ontario The BNFN negotiated and signed a treaty surrendering their traditional land to the settler federal government in exchange for or an equal share of the profits gained from forestry, mining, and fishing. The 1850 treaty was not lived up to by the federal and provincial settler governments. The result was enrichment for the former and impoverishment for the latter for over one hundred years. During this period, intergenerational trauma associated with poverty, unemployment, addiction, suicide, and family violence was experienced by this First Nation, while intergenerational prosperity was experienced by settler colonialists.

The traditional values of the BNFN include wisdom, honesty, truth, respect for the land, and *mino-bimaadiziwin*—the good life (Dempsey 2023, p. IN2). In 2018, litigation ended with the court ruling in favor of the Biigtigong Nishaabeg. The amount of money awarded to them has yet to be determined. If it approximates the $126 billion they asked the court to award them, "the good life" will have been achieved by this First Nation, and a precedent will have been set for other First Nations experiencing treaty violations by contemporary settler colonial federal and provincial governments.

A Domestic Violence Fatality Review Team is in the process of being established in Alaska. This state has the highest relative rate of Native Americans (19.7%), and a murder rate involving American Indian and Alaska Native women as victims that is ten times higher than the murder rate for the United States (Petrovsky, 2021). However, the Alaskan FRT is not being established and operated by indigenous peoples but by the Alaska Department of Public Safety.

A blended DVDRC model has not yet been implemented in Nunavut, or the other two very remote northern Canadian Territories. The problems and prospects of establishing a DVDRC in Nunavut are discussed in the next two sections.

PROBLEMS

Three problems come to mind. One is the opposition to the blended model by prominent settler colonization theorists such as Holmes and Hunt (2017, pp. 51–52). These activist-theorists recommended, "six principles to inform future indigenous family violence [prevention] initiatives." The third principle states "foster self-determination of individuals, families and communities." Implementation of this principle requires "lessening the involvement of state agencies in Indigenous people's homes, lives and communities."

Three responses to the implementation of this principle follow. First, supporters of the blended model would respond to Holmes and Hunt by pointing out the contradiction between simultaneously advocating for the principle of self-determination and limiting the ability of a Nunavut DVDRC to determine for themselves whether it should or should not seek resources from a federal government willing to provide them. Consequently, they can make their own decisions about Canadian state involvement in funding broad socio-legal changes in law, law enforcement, affordable housing, transportation, health and wellness resources, financial security, child-care support, education, and employment opportunities that "combat DV and domestic homicide" (Government of Canada, 2014; Johnson et al., 2019, pp. 13–14).

Second, a blended DVDR established for the first time in Nunavut is unlikely to achieve outcomes such as preventing family violence and femicide that a DVDR operating in a southern Canadian city for over 20 years does not appear to be able to achieve. Supporters for the establishment of a blended DVDR in Nunavut would respond by pointing out that the non-indigenous DVDRC established in Ontario is being replaced by an indigenous DVDRC in Nunavut that would be established and operated by indigenous peoples for indigenous peoples.

Third, establishing a DVDRC in Nunavut is redundant because the non-indigenous DVDRC located in a province south of Nunavut (Ontario), includes representatives of three different indigenous communities in this province. Supporters of establishing DVDRC in Nunavut would respond by stating that indigenous communities are culturally diverse. Basic quality of life needs of indigenous peoples residing in accessible, remote, and very remote communities also vary. Representatives of non-indigenous communities in Ontario do not represent the Inuit peoples residing in the very remote First Nation of Nunavut.

PROSPECTS

The prospects for establishing a DVDRC Nunavut are increased by the co-presence of a number of factors that reveal progress toward increasing the power, control, independence, and autonomy of Nunavut (Crawford, 2014). More recent changes promoting changes in the direction of promoting the achievement of these objectives are described in the paragraphs that follow.

First, federal government support for self-determination by indigenous First Nations peoples is increasing. Evidence cited by Coates (2008, pp. 16–18) reveals several steps taken by the federal government in the direction of promoting the process of Aboriginal self-government. The specific means to this end include constitutionally protected settlement agreements between indigenous peoples and the government of Canada. One consequence of these agreements is the presence in Canada today of "many Aboriginal governments that "have reconstituted themselves along traditional lines, re-establishing the control of clans, recognizing the authority of elders, and/or permitting the exercise of Aboriginal customary law . . . local control of land and . . . managing their own resources," and by extension, establishing their own DVDRC in Nunavut.

Second, in 2023, the Governments of Canada and Nunavut signed two bilateral agreements "to end gender-based violence" in Nunavut. To this end, they invested up to 16.4 million dollars to support the implementation of the National Action Plan to End Gender-based Violence in Nunavut by, among other things, "knowledge sharing, awareness campaigns and understanding its root causes" rooted in colonialism" (2023, pp. 1–2). The blended DVDRC model is designed to achieve these outcomes. As this chapter is being written, the federal government is funding decolonizing agreements that facilitate First Nations control over reserve lands and resources. Taken together, these agreements relinquish colonial control over First Nations peoples by the Indian Act (SpearChief-Morris, 2024a, 2024b).

A Government of Canada (2021) publication drew attention to steps taken in Nunavut to implement the National Action Plan (2022). The steps taken included: legislative responses (Family Abuse Intervention Act) aimed at promoting "the immediate need for safety via Family Violence Shelters, Community Safe Homes; the Child and Family Services Act, making it mandatory for all residents of Nunavut to report suspected case of child abuse; the Saillivik Program aimed at protection and support for victims of family violence prosecution policy placing "primary responsibility for decision making with the police rather than victims of male partner violence; and Abuse Partner, Parent education/information programs and "Other services," provided by the Baffin Correctional Centre, the Department of Health and Social Services, Domestic violence courts. Public prosecutors are also asked to administer "risk Assessment Tools/ Checklists "when dealing with reports of domestic violence and witnesses/victims of domestic assault." In the 2021 Government of Canada interagency publication, collaboration is conceived of as being essential for the prevention of family violence in Nunavut.

The rationale for identifying the variety of organizations and agencies described here is that they do not include an agency whose primary objective is to prevent family violence and femicide by facilitating communication, collaboration, and coordinated interventions between them. This finding provides space for the establishment of a DVDRC in Nunavut.

Second, the inclusion of settler colonization theory in the blended DVDRC established in Nunavut means that effective "decolonizing recommendations" aimed at preventing family violence and femicide can be derived from this theory. Findings reported by Chandler and Lalonde (1998, p. 1) support this hypothesis for youth suicide prevention in indigenous communities. For Paradies (2016, p. 90) these findings describe "decolonizing as endurance/recovery and its link to improved Indigenous health control," including the prevention of suicide.

Across the 200 indigenous communities, studied by Chandler and Lalonde (1998, p. 1), youth suicide rates varied between 800 times the national average and zero. Cultural continuity helped explain this finding. Cultural continuity was measured by the presence of cultural continuity factors—including pursuing land claims, self-government, control over policing, education, and cultural facilities. They found youth suicide rate for indigenous communities with zero cultural continuity factors was 69 times higher than the rate for communities where all six factors were present (138 versus 2 per 100,000). Ten years later, these findings were replicated by Lalonde.

These findings provide tentative support for the conclusion that cultural continuity is a decolonizing protective factor for youth suicides in indigenous communities. Support is tentative because other factors that could also help explain the finding of much higher youth suicide rates in "no cultural continuity indigenous communities" (e.g., greater family trauma caused by a higher proportion of parents coerced to attend residential schools) were not taken into account.

The findings reported by Chandler and Lalonde, plus the establishment of organizations such as the Inuit Broadcasting Corporation, Regional Inuit Associations and the Nunavut Land Claims Agreement were interpreted by Paradies (2016) as describing "decolonization as endurance/recovery and its link to improved Indigenous health" (p. 90).

Third, support for establishing a blended DVDRC model in Nunavut is increased by the inclusion of theories that complement each other. For example, settler colonialism theory cannot explain why some indigenous women, but not others, are killed by their male partners, and/or, why some male partners, but not others, kill them (Brownridge, 2008, p. 356). This deficit can be addressed by DVDRC recommendations derived from ecological theory because this theory is designed to explain individual and relationship differences in the perpetration of family violence and femicide.

Fourth, gender inequality is identified as a root cause of male partner violence and femicide by Women and Gender Equality Canada (2023). The inclusion of patriarchy theory in the blended DVDRC model provides a basis for deriving recommendations aimed at promoting gender equality in Nunavut.

LESSONS LEARNED

Among the many lessons that can be learned, three of the most significant are presented here. First, DVDRs established in non-indigenous communities are not appropriate for their establishment in indigenous communities. Second, by facilitating self-determination, the contemporary Canadian settler colonial federal government is creating circumstances favorable to the establishment of DVDRs in indigenous communities. Third, decolonizing interventions are likely to be included among the most effective family violence and femicide-decreasing recommendations made by DVDRs established in indigenous communities.

8

✛

Case Studies

This chapter is devoted to describing and evaluating three DVDRs with respect to the composition of their advisory groups (panels, committees, and teams), purposes, risk assessment and management, and recommendations.

The three DVDRs reviewed in this chapter are the DHR initiated by the West Berkshire Safer Communities Partnership, the Ontario DVDRC, and the Santa Clara County FRT. These three DVDRs were selected because they were the longest-running DVDRs in three different countries, the only DVDRs for which Annual Reports for the same years were available to be reviewed, and were located in three different settings—Attorney General, OCC, and the community. These three DVDRs are reviewed in the order in which they were identified.

THE WEST BERKSHIRE SAFER COMMUNITIES PARTNERSHIP (SCP/DHR)

West Berkshire (pronounced Barkshire) is part of the county of Berkshire located about 40 miles west of London, England. Since 2011, there has been a statutory requirement for local areas in England and Wales to conduct a DHR following a domestic homicide that meets the criteria set out in the Home Office Statutory guidance for the Conduct of Domestic Homicide Reviews 2011, and later 2016.

An example of how Home Office defines homicide follows:

Adult A was a 30-year-old married woman who lived with her husband Adult B at their rented home in Reading. The couple had two children. They were described as childhood sweethearts. Adult A had a job working in a local pharmacy and Adult B worked repairing street lightening. The couple moved to their rented housing property in May 2017. Adult A had a brief history of anxiety and Adult B had a lengthy history of drug misuse, primarily cocaine. He had used the drug since the age of 19 but this was not known to his wife until very soon before she was killed. It is believed the couple had a reasonable relationship and the school and GPs who had contact with both of them reported they seemed a happy couple. However, it is believed that there were arguments between them, though there was no indication that these had ever been violent. The arguments have been described as low-level bickering but nothing out of the ordinary. In the days leading up to her murder, Adult A and Adult B had a period of sustained argument, including on the night of her murder, Adult A sending her husband a series of messages via mobile phone that related to her distrust of him and her concern about his drug use. Some time on a night in November 2017, it is understood that the couple had an argument. At Adult B's trial, it was alleged that during the row Adult B attacked Adult A physically, punching her repeatedly and then strangling her. The injuries she received led to her death. A family member who visited the house found her body.

The DHRs investigated in this chapter were set up by the West Berkshire Council on behalf of the West Berkshire SCP. The West Berkshire SCP is responsible for commissioning and monitoring the DHR investigated in this chapter. Under the Police and Justice ACT 2006, SCPs are accountable to "local overview and scrutiny committees," but accountability does not entail culpability. The multi-agency panels conducting DHR reviews are said to be independent of outside influences. Representatives of Thames Valley Police (TVP) and other service providers who may have been directly or indirectly implicated in the homicide case being reviewed are not supposed to be influenced by the fact they are members of the same police force when they contribute to review panel deliberations resulting in recommendations.

Many victims and perpetrators of the homicides reviewed by DHRs were known to have contacted or were involved with multiple community-based organizations and agencies that provided support and services to them. At the same time, an unknown number of them did not contact any agency or organization. In all of the DHR reports reviewed in this chapter acronyms or contractions are used to refer to many organizations and agencies. The titles and acronyms or contractions used in the text are described here.

A2 Dominion Domestic Abuse Council (A2 Dominion)
Sovereign Housing Association (SHA)

Multi Agency Risk Assessment Committee (MARAC)
Berkshire Healthcare NHS Foundation Trust (BHFT)
Community Mental Health Team (CHMT)
Common Point of Entry (CPE)
West Berkshire Adult Social Care (WBASC)
Thames Valley Police (TVP)
West Berkshire Council Children and Family Service (WBCCFS)
Swanswell Drug and Alcohol Service (Swanswell)
General Practitioners (GPs)
Priority Group (hospital-based mental health provider)
Domestic Abuse Investigative Unit (DAIU)
National Probation Service (NPS)
Individual Management Reviews (IMR)
IRiS (Adult Drug and Alcohol Service)

Four comments about this list are warranted. One, the voices of statutory agency representatives carry more weight in review panel deliberations because they greatly outnumber representatives of voluntary agencies in all four DHR review panels. Two, one or more of the listed agencies are also contributors to the four DHRs. Three, panel review members who contribute to the DHRs are "independent and had [have] no previous involvement with subjects of the DHR" (2018 Report, s8). The apparent contradiction between being independent and a contributor was not discussed or resolved.

More generally, the DHRs reviewed in this chapter share some attributes with FRTs and DVDRCs and possess others that differentiate them from FRTs and DVDRCs in ways that make them worthy of emulation by the latter two DVDRs.

Shared attributes include confidentiality, gender neutrality—indicated by naming femicides as homicides—facilitating information sharing within and between organizations and agencies, assessing and managing risk, and making recommendations. Factors that simultaneously differentiate and elevate DHRs relative to FRTs and DVDRCs include five process factors. One, hiring an independent Chair of review panels. Two, facilitating system change by adopting a preliminary scoping process to identify organizations and agencies perpetrators and victims may have contacted or been involved with. Three, conducting an Individual Management Review (IMR) to determine if they were contacted, the nature of the contact, and their response to the contact with respect to services and interventions they may have provided. The IMR was also used to identify "improvements for future practice" and "assess the changes were made in the direction of 'better meeting the needs of individuals at risk of, or subjected to domestic abuse" (DHR Report, 2018, p. 7).

Four, survivors of intimate partner abuse and families of victims were integrated into the DHR instead of being exclusively used to identify risk factors for past femicides by DVDRCs, and not simply identified as sources of information in FRT Annual Reports. Advantages of integration include: obtaining information not included in official police and healthcare statistics (use of coercive controlling tactics, intimate partner violence); identifying barriers to services and support faced by victims and perpetrators; knowledge about why interventions made by some community-based organizations and agencies were helpful but others were not; a broader understanding of the circumstances of the femicide; supporting a more democratic homicide review process by promoting professionals, including family or survivors as equals in the voices heard during the review process (UNODC, 2023, p. 21).

The four DHR Reports reviewed in the pages that follow represent "all the DHR reports on file" with the CPS. The first DHR Report on the homicides of Julia Pemberton and her son William by the husband from whom she was separated was published in 2008. The second DHR Report on the homicide of SH (white British female) by Adult B (white British male) was published in 2016. The third DHR Report on the homicide of Karen by her husband Martin was published in 2018. The fourth and final DHR report on the murder of Adult A (white British female) by her husband Adult B (white British male) was published in 2020.

Composition

The review panel is referred to on page 21 of the 2008 DHR report but the members of the panel were not identified. Panel review members were identified in the 2016, 2018, and 2020 DHR Reports. The agencies they represented in these years varied with respect to the agencies listed earlier. In 2016 representatives of six statutory agencies were listed. They included a representative of the TVP, three representatives of West Berkshire the Regional Directors of Sovereign Housing, and a service manager for A2 Dominion Abuse Service.

In 2018 three representatives of the TVP were included among the 15-member review panel, which also included four members of West Berkshire statutory agencies and two new representatives and two new representatives of the probation service, A2 Dominion Domestic Abuse Service, and the Royal Berkshire Hospital. The 2020 DHR report listed representatives of nine agencies. Eight of the nine members of the panel review were representatives of West Berkshire.

Differences in the composition of the DHRs in different years reflect differences in the nature and frequency of contacts made with different criminal justice, civil justice, mental healthcare, physical healthcare, social care, housing, substance abuse agencies, and professionals such GPs. In the 2008 Report, the review panel concluded that three agencies—TVP, BHFT, and PCT—bore significant responsibility for the Pemberton homicides, but many other agencies were also contacted by Julia, her family, and friends.

Purposes

Three purposes are revealed by a review of DHRs identified in the 2008, 2016, 2018, and 2020 reports. One is the prevention of femicide. In the 2008 report this purpose is stated as a question—"whether the Pemberton homicides were predictable and preventable." No question about it in the 2016, 2018, and 2020 DHRs. In all of them, the listed purposes of DHRs included "the prevention of domestic violence and homicide."

Two, lessons learned by DHR reviews of homicide cases can be used to prevent family violence and femicide by applying them to improve communication and collaboration within and between community-based services to victims and perpetrators of family violence and the coordination of steps taken to prevent these adverse health outcomes.

Three, "examine the past to identify any relevant background or trail of abuse before the homicide whether support was accessed within the community and whether there were any barriers to accessing support." This purpose was added to purposes one and two that the 2020 DHR shared with the three earlier DHRs. All four DHRs also share the purpose of not finding any agency culpable for any and all actions taken and not taken, that resulted in the homicide of any person because this was held to be "a matter for the courts."

Also, barriers to accessing services are identified as a purpose, but no evidence is cited revealing the presence of barriers to specific protection services (e.g., women's shelters) or prevention services (e.g., family violence programs).

With respect to the shared purpose of "predicting and preventing femicides" there are at least two reasons why consideration should be given for excluding it from the list of stated DHR purposes. One, current statutory guidelines for conducting DHRs published by the British Home Office (2016) do not include this purpose in its list of the purposes of DHRs. Two, due to time, funding, motivation, and relevant expertise constraints, review panels do not conduct field studies aimed at isolating the independent effect of review panel recommendations on femicide or hire consultants to conduct such studies.

In the segment on purposes, lessons learned are a means to an end. In this segment lessons learned appear to be conceived of as an end in themselves. The 2008 report does not include a segment under the heading

"Lessons Learned." However, 56 "Key themes learned [from reviewing the Pemberton homicides] which need to inform future service development" by the West Berkshire Council (WBC), TVP, health professionals, and all agencies and professionals. Socially significant lessons learned include:

- Greater consideration should be given by professional organizations to the issue of information sharing in the assessment and management of evidence-based risk;
- Current legislation should be amended with a view to making it a positive duty to share information in cases where a potential threat or risk is disclosed;
- Threats to kill and suicidal inclinations should always be treated as high risk by police officers;
- Professional curiosity and routine inquiry on domestic abuse and violence should characterize interactions between GPs and their patients in all cases where relationship problems are suspected or disclosed;
- Notwithstanding the professional ethic mandating confidentiality, evidence of physical violence and the use of coercive control tactics should be communicated to the police and other healthcare agencies;
- Where persons are not in regular or sustained contact with public services, further work is needed to embed the concept of routine inquiry about the relationships between intimate partners in the daily practice of professionals, not only in health and social services but also in other voluntary organizations and agencies.

A review of the lessons learned by the DHR review panels indicates that the lesson-learning process is cumulative. As the lessons learned in earlier years contribute to the corpus of DHR knowledge on each of the topics about which lessons were learned, the 2020 review panel will have learned lessons about a greater variety of topics than their earlier counterparts. For example, lessons learned about the importance of professional curiosity about domestic violence and routine inquiry by healthcare professionals were added to the lessons learned about information sharing by GPs by 2018 DHR panel members. At the same time review panels in all four DHRs will have learned that learning lessons is one thing, and applying them is another.

Risk Assessment and Management

In 2009, a standardized risk assessment instrument named DASH (Domestic Abuse, Sexual Assault Homicide and Honour Based Violence) was created for the purpose of identifying, assessing, and managing the risk of these specific types of violence. In 2009, DASH was rolled out for use by police officers in England and Wales, including West Berkshire. The deployment of DASH ended the DHR search for a multi-agency-created risk assessment instrument. Unfortunately, none of the lessons learned by the 2016, 2018, and 2020 DHRs was about the importance and relevance of information on risk identification, assessment, and management published by social science researchers since DASH was rolled out. The attempt to close this gap follows.

The first gap-closing lesson to be learned is that risk management is the final phase of a process that begins with a multidimensional definition of risk. Building on the contribution of Myhill and Hohl (2016) risk in this chapter is conceived of as a complex concept that includes three common or underlying elements. One, situations may result in harm, individuals may cause harm, and locations in which harm are likely to occur. Two, the present probability is that harm may be perpetrated. Three, the future probability is that harm will be perpetrated. Generally speaking, the more similar the elements in the present are to those in the future, the greater the probability that harm will be perpetrated in the future.

The second valuable lesson is that accessing social science findings on the police use of DASH will help police officers, practitioners, and professionals increase the effectiveness of risk management by producing more reliable and valid risk assessments. For example, in the 2008 Report (s.82), members of the review panel learned that police officers responding to emergency calls were grading risk inappropriately by using the perceived imminence of harm as the most important risk factor because imminent harm does not predict future harm. Instead, information about a partner's historical conduct toward an intimate partner and others should have been used to assess and grade risk. However, findings reported by social science researchers indicate that the perception of imminent harm can be appropriately used to prevent future harm by police officer referrals to women's shelters or other residences in undisclosed locations (Ellis et al., 2015).

The 2008 DHR review panel did not report conclusions. Instead, the panel "drew together forty key themes" needed to inform future services provided by many, if not most of the agencies listed earlier. The noteworthy themes listed next are scattered among the themes they refer to.

- Current legislation should include a provision requiring agencies to share information with other agencies especially in potentially high-risk cases;
- The effective identification, assessment, and management of requires the use of a single multi-agency framework;

- The police response to victims of domestic violence should be guided by a framework based on a force-wide policy, procedures, and training for all officers and staff;
- Threats to kill and strangulation attempts should always be considered reliable indicators of femicide by GPs and other healthcare professionals.

In the 2016 report, five "conclusions" are described in such a way as to make it difficult to classify them as conclusions. However, in homicide case s 4.1.1, the DHR review panel concluded that despite the perpetrator's worsening risk, in the context of the perpetrator's worsening anxiety and depression, the potential for physical harm toward the victim (SH) could have been predicted, and steps could have been taken to prevent it. Because there was nothing in the perpetrator's presentation in the period leading to the death of SH's death that indicated Adult A was likely to kill her, the panel concluded that her death was neither accurately predictable nor preventable. This conclusion was contested in a British Home Office letter agreeing with the family of SH that this homicide was predictable and preventable.

The 2018 review panel also concluded that the BHFT falsely assumed that Karen was a protective factor for her partner Martin who murdered her by not fully cooperating with the police, minimizing his behavior, leaving, and then returning to live with him. Apart from opening the BHFT to allegations of victim blaming, this assumption may have been partly responsible for shoddy risk assessment by BHFT staff. This review panel also concluded that the risk assessment conducted by the National Probation Service staff was also shoddy and that the GP involved in the case did not routinely inquire about the relationship between Martin and Karen.

The 2020 review panel included the publication of 25 case-specific conclusions and the following overriding conclusion: agency staff demonstrated a lack of professional curiosity about the relationship between Adult A and Adult B. Specifically, they noted the lack of:

- Professional curiosity and routine inquiry by professionals and practitioners;
- Information sharing among organizations and agencies;
- Effective risk assessment by professionals and practitioners.

Recommendations

The 2008 review made 31 recommendations. Eight of the most socially significant and practically important recommendations were:

- The nature and scope of family involvement in the DHR process needs to be clearly established at the earliest opportunity and at all stage of the process;
- National Health Service and Home Office review the impact of conflicting requirements of confidentiality and the Duty of Candour in the context of conducting DHRs;
- Statutory agencies engaged in this DRR should work together to ensure that current protocols for information sharing among themselves and with commissioned agencies are workable, robust, and used routinely;
- Work should be undertaken to ensure that practitioners in the agencies involved in this DHR better understand the nature of protective factors in relationships and are thus well-educated to make accurate and sound judgments about those factors.
- GPs should be reminded of the necessity to make routine inquiries about domestic abuse.

With respect to the impact of recommendations produced by DHR deliberations, Boughton (2021) found that "too many repetitive findings year after year [and] not knowing the impact they have on system change and femicide rates" (p. 252) frustrates and adversely affects the motivation of advisory panel members who make them. One practice implication that can be drawn from these findings is to follow the lead set by Ohio. The Ohio FRT requires feedback on implementation and/ or coordinated interventions from selected organizations and agencies to whom mandatory recommendations are aimed at victims at high risk of being killed by male partners.

Ongoing Concerns

Five of them are noteworthy. One, in total, 87 recommendations were made by the 2008, 2016, 2018, and 2020 review panels, but none of the reports they published included information on how many recommendations were implemented, and the impact they had on increasing intra- and interagency information sharing and preventing family violence and femicides.

Two, crime statistics for West Berkshire published by the TVP indicate for every homicide (n=3 between 2018 and 2020), they reported 437 violent crimes against the person (n=2,184) that resulted in injuries (n=2,184). The ratio for homicide/criminal harassment is 469:1 (n=5/ n=2,344). None of these statistics are as startling as the ratio between the criminal offense of coercive control and homicide (0:5). Even if all three homicides involved the murder or manslaughter of females by their male partners, a reader must assume that one of the most reliable predictors of male partner perpetrators of femicide—ongoing use of coercive control tactics—was not identified as a precursor for any of the homicide cases they reviewed.

Three, the DHRs reviewed in this chapter are required to conduct all homicide reviews that are defined as homicides in British Home Office (2016) guidelines for conducting DHRs. So, in the year in which there were two or more homicides that met the criteria, the review panel must review all of them, or report differences in the "types of situations preceding the homicide selected" (e.g., victim had no contact with any agencies, homicide appears to have implications or reputation issues for a range of agencies and professionals) that describe why the homicide case was selected. The rationale for selecting cases for review was not explicitly stated in any of the DHR reports beyond stating that the case met the definition of homicide in statutory guidelines.

Four, defining all killings of women by men as homicides is not a valid definition of the homicides reviewed by all four DHRs because all the perpetrators were men, and all the victims were women.

ONTARIO DOMESTIC VIOLENCE DEATH REVIEW COMMITTEE

The Ontario Domestic Violence Death Review Committee (DVDRC) is part of the OCC of Ontario and conducts death investigations following guidelines set out in the Ontario Coroners Act, R.S.O 1990,c. C37. Two points worthy of note follow. First, when the Chief Coroners of Ontario "speak for the dead to protect the living," the victims of homicide for whom they speak are—in the vast majority of cases—victims of femicide. As part of the OCC, DVDRCs review only homicide cases referred to it by the OCC. In over 95% of the homicides they review, the victims are women.

Second, the Coroners Act requires the OCC to investigate "unnatural deaths" as well as other deaths that occur in specified locations or circumstances. Consequently, persons who survived attempts to kill them (e.g., victims of attempted murders) are not investigated by the OCC. For the first time in its history, the chair of the 2016 DVDRC authorized the investigation of "other deaths where the victim was the perpetrator's current or former partner, and the intended victims did not die," and made recommendations appropriate for them (p. 4). Successive DVDRC chairs do not appear to have exercised their discretion to review attempted femicides or homicides where the only difference between life and death may have been prompt medical attention.

Two cases that are consistent with the Ontario DVDRC definition of domestic violence-related homicide follow:

Case 2018-06 involves the homicide of a 35-year-old man by his 41-year-old female partner. There has been a history of domestic violence between the couple, including instances where the victim assaulted the perpetrator, Alcohol was a significant factor in their relationship. Five risk factors for intimate partner homicide were identified.

Case 2018-03 involves the homicide of a 31-year-old woman by her 29-year-old husband from an arranged marriage. The perpetrator was a recent immigrant and had difficulty adjusting to Canadian culture. One risk factor for intimate partner homicide was present.

The starting point for reviewing the West Berkshire DHR was the list of named organizations and agencies victims and perpetrators contacted or were involved with. Although the population of Ontario is significantly larger (12 million in 2002 to 15 million in 2020 versus 154,000 in 2008 to 161,500 in 2020), the different types of organizations and agencies contacted by victims and perpetrators do not appear to be significantly different. What is significantly different is that the named agencies contacted are identified in descriptions of DHR homicide case reviews but not in the descriptions of the homicide cases reviewed by the Ontario DVDRC.

Homicide cases reviewed by the DVDRC are described in annual reports. In this chapter, their reports are reviewed with a view to describing and evaluating progress made toward achieving stated DVDRC purposes in the year in which it was established (2003), and for three later years. Progress toward the achievement of stated purposes by the Ontario DVDRC is assessed on the basis of an investigation of the same dimensions used to investigate the West Berkshire DHR. The dimensions are composition, purposes, risk management, lessons learned, conclusions, and recommendations.

Composition

All DVDRCs include an Executive Lead, Committee Management, OCC, and most of them include a regional coroner or Chief Coroner as Chair. Domestic violence experts such as coroners/healthcare professionals, criminal justice system personnel, victim services, social workers, women's shelter staff, advocates for women, and academics. In all four years the Ontario DVDRC included more women than men. In 2023, the recently appointed chair of the DVDRC changed the composition of the Ontario DVDRC by selecting a more ethnically diverse group that included female members of three different indigenous communities to represent First Nations peoples in Ontario. Francophone, Portuguese, South Asian, and Afro-American members and a practitioner with expertise in "engaging men and boys in promoting gender equality and healthy masculinities" were also included in the 2022 DVDRC.

Between 2003 and 2022 the most significant trend in the composition of the Ontario DVDRC was the replacement of representatives of police forces by female representatives of diverse ethnic communities. In 2022, the selection of a person with expertise in promoting gender equality and healthy masculinities may result in recommendations that help change public discourse from "Why doesn't she leave her abusive male partner?" to "Why doesn't he stop coercively controlling and beating her?"

Purposes

Purposes and a mandate are identified in DVDRC annual reports. The mandate authorizes the DVDRC "to assist the OCC in the investigation and review of deaths that occur as a result of domestic violence, and to make recommendations to help prevent further deaths in similar circumstances." Purposes represent intentions to achieve specified outcomes.

In the 2002 Annual Report, members of the DVDRC intended to achieve five objectives. All of them are included in the eight purposes stated in the 2016, 2018, and 2019–2020 Annual Reports:

1. To provide and coordinate a confidential multi-disciplinary review of DV deaths pursuant to Section 15(4) of the Coroner's Act;
2. Offer expert opinion to the Chief Coroner regarding the circumstances of the events leading to the death in individual cases and their circumstances;
3. Help identify the presence or absence of systemic issues, problems, gaps, of each case to facilitate appropriate recommendations for prevention;
4. Conduct and promote research where appropriate;
5. To stimulate educational activities through the recognition of systemic problems;
6. Referral to appropriate agencies for action;
7. Where appropriate, assist in the development of protocols with a view to prevention;
8. To report annually to the Chief Coroner the trends, risk factors, and patterns identified and appropriate recommendations for preventing deaths in similar circumstances based on aggregate data collected from DVDR reviews.

A caveat attached to attempts to achieve these purposes states they are subject to limitations imposed by Coroner's Act and Freedom of Information and Privacy Act.

The relationship between intentions and outcomes may be assessed by reviewing the 2018 Annual Report. This report was selected because it is one of the most recent and detailed DVDRC annual reports (n=51 pages) on a relatively large number of homicide cases reviewed in 2017 (n=18).

Findings based on a review of the 2018 Report indicate that all the outcomes were met with the exception of "Conduct and promote research where appropriate." Specifically, readers of the 2018 Report will learn that 390 homicide cases (280 homicides and 110 homicide-suicides) domestic-violence-related homicides were recorded, and that 18 of the 20 recorded homicides were reviewed by the DVDRC.

The range between the highest and lowest yearly rate was 18 (36 in 2006 and 18 in 2014), and the ratio of victims to homicides was 1.4:1. Readers who want to learn about risk factors for lethality and the frequency of common risk factors in homicide cases reviewed between 2003 and 2019–2020 will discover answers to some of their questions in the segment that follows.

Increasing public awareness of family violence and risk factors for femicide by the publication of annual reports over the past 20 years has increased public awareness of family violence and the presence of risk factors for femicide, but not awareness of the specific organizations and agencies involved in the homicide cases reviewed by the DVDRC.

For example, specific alcohol treatment interventions, mental health programs, police force, or criminal court are not identified in the following homicide:

Throughout their marriage there was considerable discord between the perpetrator and his estranged wife, largely due to his alcohol abuse problem which traced back to his teens. They were married in 1978 and had two children. He was physically and emotionally abusive to his wife and children throughout the marriage. He had a prior criminal record and was convicted of assault—the victim of the assault was his wife. He was also a very possessive and jealous person who tried to isolate his wife and restrict her contact with family and friends, and also control her movements. He was under treatment for depression and receiving antidepression medication. His wife, at the suggestion of their family physician, tried to engage him in family counseling, however it failed when he became aggressive and angry during his final session, claiming the counselor was taking her side. Shortly after that he assaulted and threatened his wife's life on the unfounded belief she was involved with another man.

Subsequent to the perpetrator's arrest and release on bail, his wife provided a lengthy statement detailing the history of domestic violence in the lives of her and her children, as well as her husband's paranoid thoughts against two male neighbors. The perpetrator killed one of them and sought out the other the night he killed his wife. After his release on bail, he continued to harass his wife and breach its conditions. Although the breach was reported to the police, he was not arrested.

He subsequently killed his wife at their matrimonial home with a shotgun in the presence of their children. Later, he went to the home of a neighbor and, using the same weapon, killed the neighbor at his front door. He then went to another residence, seeking to kill another man, but was prevented from doing so by the other man's elderly parents. The perpetrator subsequently died in a motor vehicle collision while in flight from the police. (Case 1: 2003 Report)

There are 43 separate municipal police forces and 165 Ontario Provincial Police (OPP) detachments serving 323 municipalities in Ontario. A subsequent recommendation was made to "police officers" to enable chiefs of all municipal police forces and detachments to assume it is not specifically aimed at their police force.

In addition to police forces, no other organizations and agencies are named in any of the homicide case descriptions included in DVDRC Annual Reports. Achievement of the purpose of increasing public awareness and safety planning suffers when information about the sequencing and patterning of victim and perpetrator contacts and involvement with different agencies—or repeated contacts with the same agency—is not included in DVDRC Annual Reports. Organizations and agencies to whom recommendations were made are included in all Annual Reports but the sequencing and patterning of victim and perpetrator contacts or involvement with them is not embedded in homicide case descriptions in a way that enables a reader to tell a listener a complete story about each case.

The Ontario DVDRC interprets risk factors as "red flags" warning of the present or future danger of homicide. The identification of multiple risk factors is deemed to be important because they "allow for enhanced assessment of the risk of lethality to determine if intervention by the criminal justice system or other community-based organizations and agencies may be necessary in order to prevent future violence and possibly death." All 41 risk factors identified by the DVDRC are equally weighted. That is to say, they are classified as being equal in their ability to predict homicide (Annual Report 2018, p. 13). The possibility that a single risk factor (e.g., attempted strangulation) may more reliably predict femicide than the presence of multiple other risk factors was not considered (Annual Report 2019–2020, p. 9).

Risk Assessment and Management

In the Ontario DVDRC, risk assessment takes the form of identifying risk factors for lethality, and recommendations are used to manage risk. The risk factor thesis states that the greater the number of risk factors, the greater the ability to predict and prevent intimate partner homicides by implementing multiple, appropriate interventions. Conversely, the fewer the number of risk factors, the lower the ability to predict and prevent homicides.

Assessment of this thesis proceeds along four lines. One, findings based on the analysis of a random probability sample of six hundred domestic-related violent incidents recorded by police officers administering the DASH risk assessment instrument indicated that "the percentage of risk factors (base rate) in which a risk factor is present" is unrelated to the item loadings of risk factors. That is to say, the weight or predictive power of risk factors for femicide does not increase with the number of risk factors present, but with the consistency of a set of risk factors with each other. For example, a police officer administering DASH during a response to an emergency call records the use of coercive controlling tactics and an assault. The former has greater weight than the assault because it is more consistent with and has a greater item loading than other risk factors in DASH, such as threats to kill, strangulation attempts, stalking, problems with the police, substance abuse, mental health problems, than the assault (Myhill & Hohl, 2016, Table 1; Ornstein & Rickne, 2013). Support for assigning greater weight to coercive control than male partner violence is provided by Johnson et al. (2019), Hart (2015), and Block (2000, p. 5), who found "the fatal or near fatal incident was the first physical violence they had experienced." Similar findings were reported by Nicolaidis et al. (2003).

A proliferation of different categories of risk factors is identified in DVDRC Annual Reports. They include "common list factors" varying between 14 and 16 published in the body of Annual Reports, and 41 factors attached in Reports as Appendices. A high risk of femicide is defined as "seven or more risk factors present." Findings presented in Table 8.1 show the percentage of risk factors present in 329 homicide cases reviewed between 2003 and 2018. Specifically, it shows seven or more risk factors were present in 231 (70%) of the homicide cases reviewed, and between zero and four risk factors were present in 94 (30%). These findings cannot be used to support the enhanced assessment of preventing future femicide claims because the impact of the number of risk factors present on femicide rates is not included in Table 8.1.

Table 8.1. Number of Risk Factors per Case—All DVDR Cases Reviewed, 2003–2018 (n=329)

Number of risk factors	Number of risk factors per case	Total case
None	4	1%
1 to 3	44	13%
4 to 6	50	15%
7 or more	251	70%

Source: DVDRC Annual Report, 2012–2020.

Moreover, the seven or more risk factors resulting in enhanced as- sessment (prediction) are not identified. They could refer to the top risk factors where the average percentage of risk factors present was 48, or the bottom seven risk factors where the average percentage of risk fac- tors present was present in fewer than 30% of the cases. Diminishment is an antonym for enhanced. The percentages of diminished and enhanced risk assessment cases reviewed between 2003 and 2018 in Ontario are presented in Figure 8.1.

Findings presented in Figure 8.1 indicate that when only four statisti- cally significant predictors of femicide—suicidal tendencies (thoughts, threats, attempts), attempted femicide via strangulation, patterned use of coercive controlling tactics, substance abuse—are present, they would be classified as diminished risk because fewer than seven of them were pres- ent. Findings reported by Glass et al. (2008) indicate that compared with a control group of abused female intimate partners who did not experience nonfatal strangulation (NFS), those who did experience NFS were 7.48 times more likely to become victims of homicide. As the Ontario DVDR did not cite findings indicating that female partners for whom more than seven risk factors were present were seven or more times likely to expe- rience femicide than those for whom fewer than seven risk factors were present, the possibility that the single risk factor of NFS may be a more reliable predictor of "high risk of femicide" cases, cannot be ruled out. At the very least, the Glass et al. (2008), finding strongly supports the

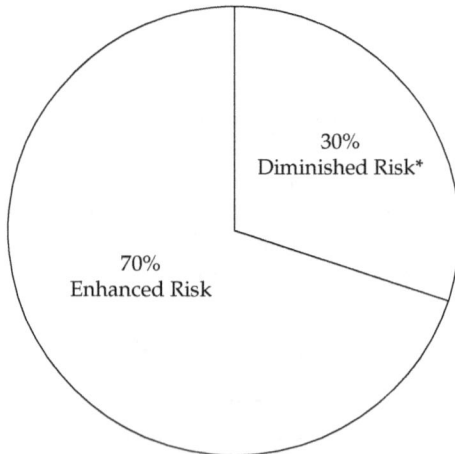

Figure 8.1. Percent of homicide cases based on numbers of risk factors per case— all DVDR cases reviewed (2003–2018). *Enhanced and Diminished Risk refers to "risk assessment, safety planning and the prevention of future deaths related to domestic violence." *Source:* DVDRC Annual Report, 2018.

inclusion of NFS among the top two or three factors for identifying high-risk femicide cases.

It is also relevant to note that in the 58 homicide cases reviewed by the Santa Clara County FRT and the West Berkshire DHR, three or fewer risk factors were identified for 47 (87%) of them. Conversely, between four and five factors were identified for seven (13%) of the homicide cases reviewed.

In Figure 8.1, separated women who experienced pre-separation male intimate partner violence would be located in the "enhanced risk of postseparation group," but Spiwak and Brownridge (2005, p. 112) found women in Canada who experienced violence while living with their ex-partner had 81% lower odds of experiencing separation violence." Moreover, when ethnicity is taken into account, differences in the risk of postseparation violence within the "enhanced risk" group are greater than the differences between the enhanced and diminished risk group. For example, there is a 40% difference between the latter two groups, but Spiwak and Brownridge (2005) found among separated women located in the same (enhanced) group, "Aboriginal women had 696% higher odds of experiencing violence than separated non-aboriginal women (p. 112).

Four, data on risk factors were collected using the Domestic History Form (DHF) which yielded "contextually specific information about actual violence, or threat of violence in a person's life" (Annual Report, 2002, p. 9). This form is not a risk assessment instrument, but a stepping-stone to the administration of a field-validated risk instrument such as the Danger Assessment 2. When the DHF was used to identify risk factors for past femicides, answers to DHF questions were provided by proxy informants, but field-validated risk assessment instruments were used to assess the risk of femicide involving contemporary female intimate partners as victims.

So, it seems that a field-validated field risk assessment instrument is used to identify risk factors for contemporary femicide cases but is not administered to survivors of attempted past femicides. If the field-validated instrument administered to contemporary female partners at high risk of experiencing femicide was also administered to survivors of past attempted femicides, it would make a more positive contribution toward preventing future femicides because the circumstances (risk factors) for past and probable future femicides would have been assessed using the same field-validated risk assessment instrument.

Three, a review of all 17 DVDRC Annual Reports published since 2003 indicates that the number of risk factors present in the homicide cases reviewed in any given year varies greatly. For example, risk factors present in the 22 of the homicide cases reviewed by the 2016 DVDRC varied between two and 23, and the 91 risk factors present in the 2018 Annual Report varied between one and 11.

The risk factor thesis states the presence of seven or more risk factors not only results in "enhanced risk assessment of femicide," but also "the prevention of future deaths related to domestic violence" (Annual Report, 2018, p. 17). The greater the number of organizations and agencies involved in a homicide case, the greater the likelihood that the need for coordinated interventions will not be met. In short, effective prevention decreases as the number of organizations and agencies to which recommendations are made increases.

Risk management is a process that is usually, if not invariably preceded by risk assessment. The use of field-validated risk assessment instruments by staff employed by professionals and practitioners providing support and services to victims and perpetrators of intimate partner violence is recommended in almost all DVDRC Annual Reports. Their use by police officers is also included in many if not most of them. Findings presented in Chapter 6 indicate that DVDRC recommendations aimed at increasing the administration of risk assessment instruments are not always followed by calculating risk scores and grading risk properly. As the recommendations are not mandatory, agency staff do not have to implement them or even acknowledge receiving them.

Recommendations aimed at increasing the administration of risk assessment instruments by police officers attending emergency (999) calls are also included in many if not most DVDRC Annual Reports because they are gatekeepers to protective services (e.g., women's shelters) where imminent harm is perceived to be highly probable, and to preventive services (e.g., programs run by advocates for women). However, the same DVDRC recommendations made to police forces repeated year after year suggests that validated risk assessment instruments are not (a) being administered, (b) interpreted in a way that identifies valid risk factors for future violence, and (c), do not locate victims in appropriate levels of risk categories for future violence during specified periods (e.g., three, six or 12 months or any time in the future).

Saxton et al. (2020, p. 1898) investigated 219 homicide cases reviewed by the Ontario DVDRC. The primary goal was to determine the number of risk factors present in "prior police contact," and "no prior police contact" homicide cases. Findings reported by these researchers revealed the "lack of formal risk assessment being completed by over one third of police contacted cases."

Saxton et al. (2020) also found victims of perpetrators with 10 or more risk factors present were significantly more likely to have had prior contact with police officers than perpetrators where fewer risk factors were present. The finding that all 219 and female victims were killed by perpetrators in both the prior contact/risk assessed and the no contract/ no risk assessment groups strongly suggests that neither the number of risk factors present, contact with police, nor the administration of a risk assessment instrument made a positive contribution to decreasing the risk of future femicides.

As the Saxton et al. (2022) study design did not include investigating the association between risk assessment and future femicides controlling the number of risk factors present, the independent effect of risk assessment on risk management could not be determined. However, findings reported by some other researchers (see Chapter 8) strongly suggest that recommendations grounded in them may not make a positive contribution to risk assessment, and consequently risk management.

What is to be done? One, findings revealing police subcultural resistance to "relationship policing" (Long et al., 2020; Wetendorf, 2021) may be decreased by changing oppositional police subcultures. Two, police officers should use risk assessment instruments to identify risk factors for imminent and future violence, and clinicians should made responsible for grading victims—locating them in ranked risk categories. Three, police officer training in domestic violence should include a segment in which they learn that arguments warrant calls for an emergency response because escalating arguments are a reliable precursor of femicide and attempted femicides (Nicolaidis et al., 2003). This recommendation is grounded in findings indicating that an unknown number of police officers believe emergency calls involving arguments are unwarranted because they are not responding to a "real" domestic violence call.

Four, absent the perceived threat of imminent harm, risk assessment instruments should be administered, and respondents should be persuaded to answer all the questions they are asked. This recommendation is grounded in findings indicating that not all questions included DASH are asked by police officers administering this risk assessment instrument in England and Wales. Recommendations about what should be done differ from the recommendations actually made by the DVDRC. These are described next.

Recommendations

Readers may recall that one of the primary goals of the DVDRC is to make recommendations aimed at "preventing deaths in similar circumstances and reducing domestic violence in general" (Annual Report, 2018, p. 30). A review of Annual Reports between 2003 and 2018 reveals that nine recurring topics figured prominently in the recommendations made between these years. This list may have educational value for readers who are not familiar with the work done by the Ontario DVDRC. All readers should note that information about (a) the impact of recommendations on each of the recurring topics, and (b) lessons learned by making recommendations on the same topic year after year is not included among the themes listed next.

1. Educating practitioners and professionals on assessing and addressing the risks associated with intimate partner violence;
2. Public education for neighbors, friends, relatives, and families of victims or potential victims;
3. Addressing issues of intimate partner violence in specific underserved populations such as ethnic and religious communities;
4. Public policies aimed at violence in workplaces, bullying and stalking, cyber and online violence;
5. Mental health impact on domestic violence;
6. Recognition and assessment of risk factors and preparing safety plans;
7. Financial and health concerns;
8. Substance abuse by victims and perpetrators;
9. Child custody, family court decisions, and child welfare concerns.

The "similar circumstances" referred to in the opening paragraph are usually risk factors for femicide. Since the establishment of the Ontario DVDRC in 2002, 41 risk factors have been identified, and over 400 recommendations were aimed at reducing homicides where similar risk factors were present in previous cases. The recommendations were made to over 30 named organizations and agencies, and hundreds of professionals and practitioners who provide support and services to potential victims and perpetrators among whom the same risk factors were present.

Any story told about the history of recommendations made by the Ontario DVDRC would have to start with the 2003 DVDRC Annual Report. In this report, recommendations made about the 11 homicide cases reviewed elicited 38 recommendations aimed at heightening and increasing awareness and education, assessment and intervention, and resources. During a span of 17 years (2003 to 2020) more than 400 recommendations were made to over 30 named government ministries, universities, schools, agents of the criminal justice system, the College of Physicians and Surgeons, family court lawyers, and hundreds of family violence prevention professionals and practitioners in Ontario. To what end?

One of the stated purposes of the Ontario DVDRC is the prevention of future femicides by making recommendations to community-based organizations and agencies. However, evidence indicating that recommendations decreased the probability of femicide in Ontario was not included in any Annual Report. For some of the years since the establishment of

the Ontario DVDRC it was possible to collect data on the number of recommendations and the number of femicides over eight years. Findings
presented in Figure 8.2 indicate that DVDRC recommendations were
unrelated to homicide rates.

In October 2022, the current DVDC chair and chief counsel to the OCC
publicly acknowledged that despite making "hundreds upon hundreds
of recommendations" aimed at preventing femicide epidemic, "the number of deaths isn't dropping." Moreover, he identified "recommendation
fatigue" (getting the same suggestions and responding the same way)
and inappropriate recommendations (inapplicable or don't actually fit the
system they're intended to fit into) as factors responsible for the failure of
organizations and agencies to respond to recommendations made to them
(Nease, 2022). The "big changes" he proposed included creating a more
ethnically diverse DVDRC that would make "novel and aspirational" recommendations instead of repeating "apathetic, unambitious and torpid"
recommendations year after year (Cross, 2023).

One way of interpreting this big change is that it reflects the need to
"think about things from a different perspective rather than just repeating them over and over again" (Cross, 2023). Another way of interpreting
it is to identify the "big change" as the last step in making the Ontario
DVDRC immune to evaluation.

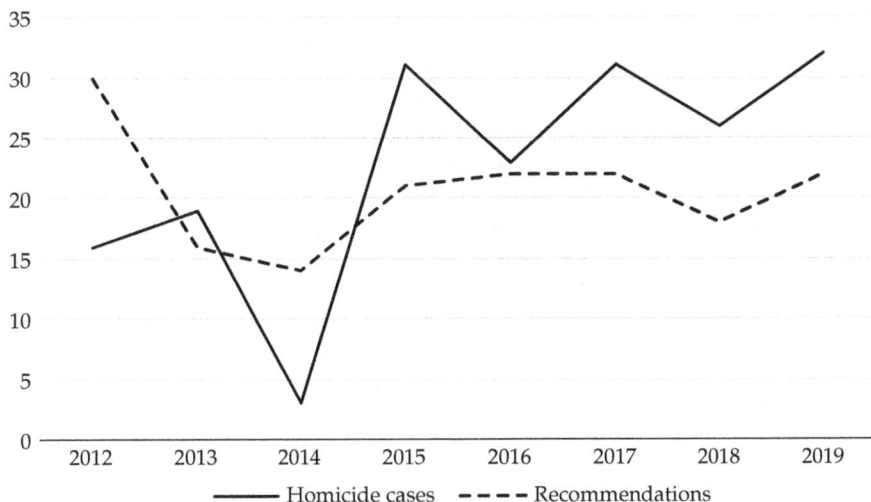

Figure 8.2. Recommendations and homicide cases. *Note.* Years selected start at 2012
because a report on the implementation of Domestic Violence Death Review Committee Recommendations, 2007–2011 was published by Action-Research-Change (2014),
Ottawa.

The first two steps taken were methodological. One, preventing femicide was defined as an "underlying" purpose whose achievement required collecting data on the root causes of femicide they were unable or unwilling to collect. Two, the inability to identify the independent effect of DVDR recommendations on femicide rates (Alvarez, 2004; Boughton, 2021; Dawson, 2021, p. 679; Home Office, 2016; UNODC, 2023, pp. 14).

The second two steps taken were substantive. First, lessons learned and system change gradually replaced preventing femicide as the primary purpose of DVDRs (Dawson, 2021; Home Office, 2016; Websdale et al., 2019, p. 4; UNODC, 2023). Second, recommendations aimed at preventing substantive outcomes such as femicide were replaced by "novel and aspirational" recommendations (Cross, 2023). In other words, preventing femicide is no longer an outcome to be achieved, but an outcome DVDRCs aspire to achieve (Cross, 2023, p. 3).

Consequently, the attention of researchers is diverted from assessing the impact of recommendations on femicide to assessing the collective strength of the aspiration to achieve this objective. Moreover, while progress toward achieving the goal of preventing femicide is fixed in time in the sense that DVDRC Annual Reports cover homicides occurring during the past 12 months, or over the past 20 years, aspirations to achieve this goal are timeless.

In addition to the finding that DVDRC recommendations defined as "torpid" by the chief coroner of Ontario did not decrease the probability femicide in Ontario, a perusal of DVDRC recommendations actually made over the past 20 years elicits two additional concerns. First, they are grounded in the unstated assumption that women prioritize leaving physically violent and abusive male partners (Campbell et al., 1998; Cavanagh, 2003; Hoyle, 2008; Peled et al., 2000). Consequently, no recommendations are aimed specifically at women who want to remain with their partners but want the violence and abuse to stop (Goodmark, 2007).

This gap is met by safety planning researchers. Preventing femicide by women who are still living with violent and abusive male partners is not a stated purpose of DVDRs (Davies, 2009; Goodkind et al., 2004; Goodman et al., 2005).

Second, the DVDRC (2022 Annual Report) recommendation that police officers implement what appears to be a "no drop charges" policy phrased as supporting reluctant victims to cooperate in the criminal justice process of charging and prosecuting alleged perpetrators of criminal violence simultaneously deprives police officers and prosecutors of their discretion, victims of agency, and replaces male partner control by state control (Goodkind et al., 2004). The alternative of recommending an evidence-based policy routinely deployed in homicide cases where the victim cannot testify is not included in any DVDRC Annual Report.

Increasing public awareness of femicide is another stated purpose of the Ontario DVDRC. As separation is included among the top two risk factors in most of the Annual Reports published by the Ontario DVDRC, information submitted to the media is aimed at increasing public awareness of separation as a precursor of femicide. However, increasing public awareness of "separating or planning to separate" from a male partner as a risk factor "present in 67/68% of homicide cases" (Gillis & Hasham, 2017)without qualification might have the unintended effect of motivating some physically abused and/or coercively controlled female partners to eschew separation in favor of continuing to reside with abusive and controlling partners, or to return to live with them if they have already separated (Mahoney, 1991).

Qualification could involve a statement to the effect that a very small subset of separated female partners—one-half of 1%—were killed by their male partners in Ontario. This finding is derived from Statistics Canada (2022) information about the average number of separations in Ontario (45,994) occurring over a number of years (2017–2020), and the average number and percentage of femicides during the same period (21 or 0.05%). Increasing the proportion of social science researchers serving as members of the Ontario DVDRC may result in more accurate or nuanced media awareness reports being submitted to the media that must always include a statement to the effect that the killing of even one woman is reprehensible and preventable.

The Auditor General of Ontario publishes annual "value for money" reports on organizations and agencies such as addiction treatment programs and adult correctional institutions in Ontario. In 2019, the Auditor General (AG) published a value for money Annual Report on the OCC. The Ontario DVDRC is part of the OCC which forwards to it homicide cases where there is reason to believe the death was related to domestic violence. In the 2018–2019 fiscal year, the OCC's total expenditure was $47 million. An unspecified percentage of these expenditures were incurred by the Ontario DVDRC. The AG review led her to conclude that the residents of Ontario were not getting full value for the taxes they contributed to operate the OCC or DVDRC.

Two other conclusions published by the AG are also worthy of note. First, the OCC "did not demonstrate that it has effective systems in place to have consistent high-quality death investigations that improve public safety and prevent or reduce the risk of preventable deaths" (Auditor General of Ontario, 2019, p. 456). Second, "Unlike other Canadian provinces the OCC does not publish government and other organizations' responses to death review committee recommendations limiting their usefulness in learning from the past to minimize the occurrence of future preventable deaths" (p. 456).

During the years in which DVDRC investigations of domestic-related homicides were being conducted, coroners paid by the OCC were "not consistently conducting high quality death investigations and staff did not sufficiently analyze data or follow up on the implementation of recommendations to improve public safety and help prevent further deaths" (Auditor General of Ontario, 2019, p. 454). This finding suggests that DVDRC homicide investigations were being conducted in a workplace context in which the OCC did not appear to value high-quality investigations that reduced the risk of preventable deaths in similar circumstances.

Two recommendations aimed at the public were also derived from the findings reported by the AG. One, the OCC should work with the Ministry of the Solicitor General to get more immediate public access to the current status of the implementation of and responses to recommendations made by the DVDRC. Two, the OCC should communicate to the public the value, benefit, and potential concerns about recommendations included in DVDRC Annual Reports. The OCC may have accepted and implemented these recommendations following the publication of the AG's Report in 2019, but it did not include information about their implementation in the 2019 or 2020 Annual DVDRC Reports.

One factor that should be taken into account in responding to findings and recommendations made by the AG is the achievement of the objective of preventing femicide is hindered by constraints placed on the DVDRC to achieve this purpose. Specifically, DVDRC recommendations aimed at implementing recommendations are not legally binding. Consequently, there is no obligation for organizations and agencies to implement or even respond to the recommendations made to them. Another factor is that information exchanges between organizations and agencies who share the objective of preventing family violence by potential perpetrators of femicide is, or may be, prohibited by provisions of the Freedom of Information and Privacy Act.

Three positive contributions made by the Ontario DVDRC were not referenced in the AG's Report. First, the Ontario DVDRC facilitated attempts of representatives of the community to solve social problems present in them. Second, by publishing Annual Reports since it was first established in 2003, the Ontario DVDRC made a positive contribution toward increasing public awareness of the prevalence of femicide and risk factors for this outcome during the past 20 years. Third, DVDRC recommendations made a positive contribution toward the administration of risk assessment instruments by professionals and practitioners in Ontario.

Since the AG's Report was published in 2019, the Ontario DVDRC has extended its reach by agreeing to investigate the egregious failure of judges, crown attorneys, defense lawyers, and police officers to prevent the murder of three women in Renfrew County following public outrage elicited by an inquest with province-wide implications.

Finally, like the Santa Clara FRT and the West Berkshire DHR, the Ontario DVDRC has never been independently evaluated since they were established over 20 years ago. Findings from this review may motivate DVDRCs in five other Canadian provinces to focus on answering the same policy-relevant question: Why are so many females being killed by their male intimate partners when, in the majority of cases, the perpetrator is known to the victim, friends, relatives, neighbors, and perhaps workmates, and risk factors for lethality have been identified (Gillis & Hasham, 2017)?

Jaffee et al. (2008) argue that an answer to this question is the creation of a national, collaborative DVDRC consistent with the Government of Canada's Family Violence Initiative. Federal support for such a project may be contingent upon persuading federal government policymakers to fund a project that (a) has not been implemented in all 10 Canadian provinces and the three territories, (b) does not cite evidence indicating that DVDRCs help prevent femicide by promoting gender equality, and (c) the residents of the province of Ontario did not get full value for the taxes they contributed to the establishment and operation of the Ontario DVDRC.

Inquests in Ontario were held long before the establishment of the Ontario DVDRC in 2003. Unlike the Ontario DVDRC, inquests in Ontario are conducted in public; held following a request by a family member, or when the public interest will be served by knowing about the specific conditions under which the homicide(s) or femicide(s) occurred; witnesses and other interested parties such as family violence prevention agencies can be given standing, present evidence and make recommendations, be cross-examined, and an inquest jury will review the evidence and make nonbinding recommendations (Mason & Cross, 2022).

Although they are presided over by a coroner, inquests are independent of the OCC of Ontario. Consequently, recommendations made by interested parties who are given standing tend to have greater substantive importance, relevance, and province-wide applicability than recommendations made by the Ontario DVDRC.

For example, recommendations made by the Culleton, Kuzyk, Warmedam Coroners (Renfrew County) Inquest Jury included: formally declaring intimate partner violence an epidemic; establish an independent Intimate Partner Violence Commission dedicated to eradicating intimate partner violence and acting as a voice that speaks on behalf of survivors and victims's families; raising public awareness; ensuring the transparency and accountability of government and other organizations for assessing IPV in all its forms; establishing a provincial implementation committee dedicated to ensuring implementation of recommendations from this inquest; amend the Coroners Act to require the recipient of an inquest recommendation to advise the OCC if a recommendation is complied with or to provide an explanation if it is not; complete a yearly review of public attitudes through public opinion research; prioritize the development of cross-agency and cross-system collaboration services; improve the coordination of services addressing substance abuse, mental health, child protection and IPV perpetration, investigate and develop a common framework for risk assessment in IPV cases which includes a common understanding of IPV and lethality; refer high risk cases to high-risk committees; study the best approach to permitting disclosure of information about a perpetrator's history of IPV and the potential risk to new and future partners who request such information; explore adding the term "femicide" and its definition to the Criminal Code. The last inquest jury recommendation was to reconvene one year following the verdict to discuss the progress made in implementing these recommendations. If all these inquest jury recommendations were implemented by the provincial government, they would come close to making the Ontario DVDRC redundant.

The Chief Coroner of Ontario was present at the Renfrew County County inquest held June 6–28, 2022. The 86 recommendations made to the provincial government by the inquest jury included one that directly impacted the OCC by recommending an amendment to the Coroners Act that would "require the recipient of an inquest recommendation to advise the Office of the Chief Coroner if a recommendation is complied with or to provide an explanation if it is not implemented (# 6)." Perhaps the chief coroner will eventually respond by supporting an amendment that also applies to recipients of DVDRC recommendations aimed at preventing femicide in high-risk femicide cases.

Every femicide is a public interest femicide, but some femicides may require a province-wide government response because they elicit greater publicity, public interest, condemnation, and safety concerns, and also involve outrageous indifference and/or egregious transgressions of law, protocols, and normative practice by police officers, prosecutors, judges, and staff employed by organizations and agencies whose purposes include preventing family violence and femicide.

For example, an inquest was held for a case in which a mother and her two young children were murdered by her estranged husband. Prior to the murders, the mother filed a domestic violence complaint with the police in Montreal alleging her estranged husband "twisted her arm, tried to bite her upon leaving a bank meeting and threatened her with scissors." The chief coroner of Quebec called for an inquest to be held on this case. Reasons for ordering the inquest included concerns raised by the coroner about how little was done by "the authorities, including the work of prosecutors and the judicial system" to prevent the murders (Canadian Press, 2023).

The evidence presented in inquests more closely approximates a trial and has greater validity than evidence cited by the Ontario DVDRC review of homicide cases. Consequently, consideration should be given to passing provincial legislation holding inquests mandatory, rather than holding them at the discretion of coroners, in all cases where (a) the domestic violence-related murder of multiple victims is perpetrated by males known to have been abusive, violent and/or coercively controlling, and (b) attempts to prevent them by agents of the criminal and civil (family) justice systems were egregiously ineffective or even complicit in them. Currently, the reverse is true. That is to say, the Ontario DVDRC has been called upon to review a notorious case (Renfrew County) for which an inquest had already been held. The rationale for this decision is unclear.

SANTA CLARA COUNTY FATALITY REVIEW TEAM

The Santa Clara Death Review Committee (DRC) was established in 1994. This committee published a final report in the same year. At some point, the name of the DRC was changed to FRT (Fatality Review Team). Access to FRT Annual Reports was published under the District Attorney's Publications and Policies website. This source published only four FRT Annual Reports 2018, 2019, 2020, and 2021. All the homicide cases reviewed by the Santa Clara FRT were adjudicated. They represent a very small fraction of the domestic violence cases referred to the Office of the District Attorney for review in the same years. Specifically, the ratio of domestic violence cases to homicide cases reviewed by the 2018 FRT was 5,519 to 7, or 788:1.

An example of a domestic violence-related homicide reviewed by the Santa Clara FRT is provided by Case #293:

> On November 18 the perpetrator and victim were heard arguing in the room they shared in the perpetrator's parents' home. The victim moved to the United States from Northern Ireland after meeting the perpetrator online and had been in the United States for approximately one year. The perpetrator shot the victim in the head and then shot himself in the head with a gun.

Results of reviewing the four Annual Reports and the Final Report published by the DRC in 1994 are presented in the pages that follow. The review focuses on the topics investigated in reviews of the Ontario DVDRC and the West Berkshire DHR.

Unlike the West Berkshire DHR but like the Ontario DVDRC, the Santa Clara FRT does not name the specific organizations and agencies contacted by victims and/or perpetrators. That is why they are not listed here. The difference in naming organizations and agencies contacted by the Santa Clara FRT and the West Berkshire DHR is revealed by the comparison that follows.

> Case 7 1994 DRC REPORT: Victim may have had a relationship with a sixteen-year-old perpetrator. He broke it off. She gets another juvenile and they kidnap the decedent using a stun gun. The other juvenile leaves before the murder. Perpetrator shoots and kills him leaving his body in the woods. He isn't found until several days later. The juvenile had numerous previous contacts with the system, she was a dependent child and a former foster child of the victim's mom. Decedent also had prior contact with the system. He had been convicted 3 years earlier of torturing animals. Perpetrator was found guilty of manslaughter, tried as an adult Caucasian.

In the Adult A and Adult B homicide case reviewed by the West Berkshire DHR (DHR 2018), the seven organizations and agencies who were involved with or contacted by the perpetrator and/or victim were named, and attention was drawn to the lack of information sharing and missed opportunities for prevention by each of them.

As noted earlier, failure to name also results in the loss of information about the sequencing and patterning of first-to-last contacts with formal and informal family violence prevention agencies and organizations. In several cases, 11 of 51 in the 1994 Report, no agency or organization was contacted but information on why they were not contacted is not included in homicide case reviews. Consequently, recommendations derived from knowledge of differences in careers ending in the death of victims and perpetrators in the contact and no contact groups cannot be made.

The decision to name organizations and agencies contacted by perpetrators and/or victims may be influenced to a greater or lesser degree by the composition of the Santa Clara FRT. Specifically, the decision not to name may simply reflect the greater persuasive power of members selected to represent organizations and agencies that do not want to be named. In other words, the decision to name or not name may be dependent upon the composition of the Santa Clara FRT.

Composition

The 17 members of the 1994 DRC included 11 representatives from criminal and law enforcement agencies, coroners, and the family court, and the remainder (n=12) represented therapeutic community-based organizations and agencies. Representatives from the latter group outnumbered representatives from the former group 20 to 15 in the 2018 FRT. Composition of the 2019 FRT was more balanced with 17 team members representing law enforcement agencies, the family court, and 18 representing community-based organizations and agencies providing therapeutic services (e.g., clergy, YWCA, Community Solutions, and Domestic Violence Intervention Collaboration). In the 2019 FRT, representatives of law enforcement agencies, coroners, and the family court were outnumbered again. Specifically, 27 of the 45 members of the FRT represented therapeutic organizations and agencies. The 2021 FRT was composed of 21 representatives of the latter group and 25 representatives of law enforcement coroners and the family court.

No clear unidirectional trend emerges from a comparison of differences in the composition of FRTs reported here. The expectation that an FRT located in the Office of the District Attorney would always include a greater number of representatives from law enforcement agencies was not met. The compositional changes in FRTs in different years may simply reflect differences in the nature of the homicide cases reviewed each year.

Purposes

The "ultimate purpose" of the 1994 DRC was to "avoid deaths in the future" without blaming community-based organizations and agencies. One of the means to this end was the signing of a confidentiality agreement by all members of the DRC. Two goals, "preventing future deaths and improving system response," were identified in the 2018 FRT Report. The stated means to these ends were recommendations based upon lessons learned from homicide reviews made to community-based organizations and agencies.

The same goals were identified in the FRT Annual Reports. The stated purpose of the FRTs was "to make recommendations aimed at preventing deaths in similar circumstances and reducing domestic violence in general." The "ultimate" purpose of the 1994 DRC—preventing femicide—became the present purpose of the 2018, 2019, 2020, and 2021 FRTs.

System change was added as a purpose in itself in the four FRTs, but it is not identified as a means of preventing femicide. Consequently, progress toward achieving system change can be assessed independently of the contribution it makes to preventing femicide. In other words, facilitating system change is an end in itself.

The search for risk factors for past femicides is not an end in itself but a means of preventing future femicides. Risk factors are conceived as "red flags" warning of danger. In the 1994 DRC Report, six risk factors were identified and ranked according to the number of homicide cases in which they were present. A comparison of the risk factors listed in the

Santa Clara FRT and Ontario DVDRC Annual Reports reveals the following interesting and practically important findings.

One, the DVDRC ranking of the 14 "common" risk factors is based on the percentage of risk factors present in the relationship between intimate partners that ended in femicide—the higher the percentage, the higher the risk. The criterion used to rank the 17 "commonly seen" risk factors in the FRT is not documented. They are simply numbered one to seventeen suggesting the higher the number, the higher the risk.

Two, the audiences for which the lists were created are different. Specifically, recommendations derived from the 17-item FRT list were "warning signs for victims," while the DVDRC list is used as a basis for making recommendations to community-based organizations and agencies.

Three, the number and variety of risk factors identified by the DVDRC increased from 18 to 41 since its establishment in 2003, whereas the number and types of risk factors included in the 2018 Annual Report are the same as the list included in the 2019, 2020, and 2021 Annual Reports.

Four, some factors included in the DVDRC list (e.g., suicide, unemployment, nonfamily violence, escalation of violence, and depression) are included in the DVDRC but not the FRT list of risk factors, and some factors included in the FRT list (e.g., "show anger that is out of proportion to the incident and becomes emotionally intense and frightening) are included in the FRT but not the DVDRC list.

Five, enumerated lists of protective factors aimed at "families and friends of domestic violence victims" are published in FRT but not DVDRC reports. Families and friends who become aware of the presence of one or more of seven enumerated risk factors (warning signs) such as "partner puts them down in from other people, constantly worried about making their partner angry, have unexplained marks or injuries, and showing signs of emotional abuse" are encouraged to refer them to protective and prevention resources available in their communities. In their relationships with female partners showing these warning signs, families and friends are encouraged to be supportive and nonjudgmental, help them prepare a safety plan, and overcome isolation by participating in activities outside the relationship. Families and friends are also advised not to "pressure a person to leave a relationship when they are not ready because it may silence victims and further isolate them." Instead, they should be a "supportive, non-controlling person they can turn to when they are ready."

Finally, one of the most significant findings revealed by a comparison of the Santa Clara FRT and the Ontario DVDRC is not about the differences between them but what they have in common. What they have in common is the failure to make recommendations aimed at community-based agencies whose mandates include liberating females from coercively controlling male partners.

Risk Assessment and Management

Between 1993 and 1997 risk was assessed based on risk factors identified by reviews of homicide cases recorded by police officers, and risk was managed by six recommendations aimed at educating the public, courts, schools, workplaces, the elderly, and obtaining restraining orders. Risk management in action is illustrated by Case 4/5.

> Husband shot wife and then himself. No prior contacts at all with the system. Arranged marriage and per police department wife may have been seeing someone else. Family members for victim believe someone else committed the murders even though evidence clearly points to murder suicide.

"No prior contacts with the system" were reported for 11 of the 51 cases and the recommendation was "public education so victims know where to turn when they are being victimized." However, this recommendation was applicable to only 11 (22%) of the 51 homicide cases reviewed by the 1994 Santa Clara DRC. Moreover, the risk management advice given to victims was based upon the presence of seventeen risk factors/red flags that are not differentiated from each other on the basis of whether the danger of femicide or life-threatening injuries is imminent or only likely to occur in the near or more distant future.

> Case 28, 1994 Report describes a homicide where immediate danger was present: Victim and defendant live together. Victim has drug problems. Defendant also using. No prior police reports of domestic violence involving these two. They argue. Defendant ends up killing her with his hands and a blunt instrument.
>
> Case 42, 1994 Report describes a homicide where future danger was present: Defendant and victim are husband and wife. Three children together. Defendant is very possessive, jealous and totally controls the victim. He is not working. She finally moves out, but only moves around the corner with the children and her dad. Their back fences touch. He continues to control her, making her come to him just about nightly. The youngest son, 7 years old goes with them on the night of the homicide. Defendant is up all night using meth. He sees a shadow on the wall, thinks it's a signal from her boyfriend, proceeds to beat her to death. She dies from his brutal beating.

In the "What Else Can Be DONE" segment of the 1994 DHC and subsequent FRT Reports risk management advice was given to family members, friends, neighbors, and coworkers on how to intervene when they become aware of "serious problems in the relationship." However, as indicated earlier, the advice given does not tell them what to do when the danger of harm is imminent and when it is likely to be experienced in the future.

In subsequent FRT Reports (2013, 2018, 2019, 2020, and 2021), 17 "warning signs for victims commonly seen in homicides and homicide-suicides and suicides" were identified, and victims were advised to reach out to advocacy groups in the community and seek their advice if their intimate partners perpetrated any of them. Manifestly, the onus is being placed on prospective victims to protect themselves. However, the advice being given to them does not vary with the ethnicity of the groups accounting for a disproportionate number of homicides and homicide suicides perpetrated in Santa Clara County. Specifically, Hispanics account for 17% of the population and 63% of the 51 cases reviewed by the Santa Clara FRT between 1993 and 2021, but culturally specific advice with respect to overcoming barriers to support services—especially child abuse prevention services, cultural legitimation of wife beating, and the use of violence to settle conflicts (Straus & Gelles, 1990, pp. 364–65)—was not included in FRT Reports.

After 2014, greater weight in assessing risk was given to a field-validated risk assessment instrument—the Lethality Assessment Screen (LAS)—designed to achieve two objectives. One is to decrease rates of repeat, severe, lethal, and near-lethal violence. Two is to increase rates of emergency safety planning and help-seeking.

Use of the LAS by Santa Clara police officers elicits four concerns. One, the LAS includes 11 questions selected from the Danger Assessment (revised). Risk grading instructions—yes and no answers that trigger protocol referrals—are included with the instrument. Police officers responding to emergency domestic violence calls are required to follow a detailed set of instructions on how to administer and interpret yes and no answers to the LAS questions by victims. Specifically, a protocol referral is automatically required by a yes answer to the first three questions. However, a negative answer to the first three questions but a positive answer to at least four of the remaining eight questions will also trigger a protocol referral. Unwillingness to answer any of the 11 questions can still trigger a protocol referral if the victim answers "yes" to the question: "Is there anything else that worries you about your safety? (If "yes") What worries you?" Or the police officer believes the victim is in a potentially lethal situation.

Why would a victim involved in a stressful situation who does not answer any of the first 11 questions be willing to answer the 12th question? Moreover, why would busy police officers attending stressful emergency domestic violence calls take the time to administer the LAS when they also have the option of asking one question, and/or making a protocol referral on the basis of their professional knowledge, experience, and intuition? One or more of these reasons may have led the authors of 2018 Santa Clara County Report to conclude that "challenges remain in the application and making sure that the LAS is used consistently."

Two, findings based on the study of a nationally representative sample of 721 Hispanic families revealed that "the rate of severe assaults on wives is more than double that of non-Hispanic white families," and the high Hispanic rates of family violence and homicide "indicate that family violence is a major threat to the integrity and well-being of Hispanic families" (Straus & Gelles, 1990, pp. 365–66). As Hispanic families were not included as a named ethnic group in any of the eight LAS study sites (police jurisdictions) selected by Messing et al. (2014, p. 34), the findings they report may not be generalizable to Santa Clara County in California. Consequently, the results of using the LAS to assess and manage the risk of family violence and femicide in Oklahoma—where it was field tested— may not be the same as when it used in Santa Clara County, California.

Three, difficulties in facilitating communication, collaboration, and coordination between social services have been an ongoing problem for FRTs, DVDRCs, and DHRs since their establishment. The LAS focuses on collaboration between the police forces and several named social services in selected jurisdictions, but not on facilitating information sharing and collaboration between the social service agencies themselves.

Three, evidence indicating the impact of the LAS on preventing femicide and attempted femicide is not included in any Santa Clara County FRT Annual Report.

Four, five protective factors were identified in the LAS (Messing et al., 2014, p. 58). They include:

- Received services related to domestic violence;
- Went some place where he couldn't find you;
- Partner went someplace where he couldn't find or see me;
- There was a period of time when I did not see my partner;
- I was treated by a doctor or nurse for injuries;
- I did something to protect myself from my partner such as mace, pepper spray, or a weapon.

Information on the contribution made to risk management by the presence of protective factors was not included in any of the Santa Clara FRT Annual Reports.

Finally, the expectation that an FRT located in the office of the Attorney General would add objectives that reflected law enforcement priorities is confirmed by the use of the LAS to (a) inform prosecutor's decisions regarding filing charges, (b) provide information helpful to the issue of custody status in cases where charges are filed, and (c) assist law enforcement in knowing which cases warrant immediate referral to a domestic violence agency (p. 15).

Recommendations

The 2018 Report includes 12 recommendations derived from a "deep dive" (in-depth analysis) of one case. One of them is a very strong recommendation endorsing the use of the LAS. This report also includes recommendations for greater education in domestic violence and the resources available to mental health system or victims, increasing awareness among professionals and practitioners of the impact of adverse childhood experiences on the perpetration of future violence. Three noteworthy recommendations were made by the Santa Clara FRT. One, assessment for traumatic brain injuries should be done in every case of intimate partner violence that results in injuries to the head. Two, law enforcement should be contacted in every case where an intimate partner is a danger to him/herself and possesses a gun, Three, referring agencies should inform law enforcement in 5150 Holds cases where a person is being involuntarily held in a mental hospital for up to 72 hours.

Except for the absence of 5150 Holds, these recommendations are replicated in the 2019, 2020, and 2021 Annual Reports.

Members of Asian communities outnumber members of all the other ethnic groups in Santa Clara County (38%) and also outnumber victims and perpetrators of the homicide cases reviewed by the 1994 DHC (33%). Yet, none of the recommendations are specifically aimed at preventing honor-based femicides involving Asian people as perpetrators and victims in the 1994 and 2018, 2019, 2020, and 2021 Reports. One reason for their absence could be that no honor-based femicides were reviewed. The 1994 Report also includes a recommendation that "all school districts develop a curriculum which addresses the issue of domestic violence." However, the opportunity to recommend "the development of healthy relationships" in the curriculum was missed" (Messing et al., 2022). It was also missed in 2018 by 2019, 2020, and 2021 FRTs. The implementation of FRT recommendations is voluntary. Information about their voluntary implementation by the organizations and agencies to whom they were made is not included in any FRT Report.

All three of the DVDRs reviewed here made recommendations, but none of them stated criteria used in making them. The Alberta, Canada, DVDRC is unique in that it uses SMART criteria (Specific, Measurable, Achievable, Realistic, Timely) for this purpose. However, a review of its Annual Reports reveals that the application of SMART does not appear to have made any impact on the number of police-reported domestic violence-related homicides reviewed by the Alberta DVDRC between 2012 and 2021. One reason for this outcome may be that recommendations aimed at preventing femicide were not included in any of the Annual Reports published during these years.

LESSONS LEARNED

Four lessons learned come to mind. One, data collection, analysis, and recommendations made by FRT, DVDRC, and DHR were not informed by theory. Two, similarities are greater than differences among the three DVDRs, but some differences present in DHRs but not the Santa Clara County FRT and the Ontario DVDR (e.g., Internal Management Review) are worthy of emulation by FRTs and DVDRCs. Three, FRTs and DV-DRCs are dominated by the quest for risk factors and the absence of the collection of data on protective factors. Three, the FRT, DVDRC, and DHR do not cite empirical evidence indicating they are fit for the purpose of preventing femicide. Four, all three DVDRs can be made fitter to achieve system change, increasing public awareness of family violence and femicide and educating professionals and practitioners in the effective use of risk assessment instruments and risk management.

CONCLUSIONS

1. FRTs, DHRs, and DVDRCs are not fit for the purpose of preventing femicide;
2. DVDRs can be made fitter for the purpose of preventing femicides and attempted femicides by establishing RDVDRs serving multiple DVDRs located in any jurisdiction (see Chapter 4).
3. The DHR is worthy of emulation by FRTs and DVDRCs;
4. Gender neutrality is a pervasive and enduring attribute of FRTs, DVDRCs, and DHRs;
5. Data collection by DVDRs is dominated by the quest for risk factors and the absence of data on protective factors for femicide;
6. Recommendations aimed at preventing homicide-suicides are not differentiated from recommendations aimed at preventing suicide-homicides;
7. Healthcare providers, especially hospital ER staff, tend to be less likely to share information relevant to preventing family violence and femicide than many, if not most community-based organizations and agencies whose purposes include prevention of these adverse health outcomes;

8. Positive contributions made by DVDRs were neglected. Positive contributions identified by UNODC (2023) include:
    - Educating the public;
    - Improved communication between courts (family and criminal) and community agencies;
    - Increased funding for services to abused women;
    - Instituted a novel data collection system for domestic violence;
    - Changed policies regarding the adoption of batterer intervention programs;
    - Promoted the adoption of specific danger assessment tools (e.g., DASH, LAS);
    - Facilitated the development and use of risk assessment instruments;
    - Facilitated the use of new screening procedures for mental health and suicide;
    - Identified over 40 risk factors for femicide;
    - Increased the involvement of civil society in social problem-solving.

Keeping the caveat stated earlier (see Chapter 4) in mind, ChatGPT T3.5 provided a four-page Artificial Intelligence "critical evaluation of fatality review teams" that concluded "FRTs play a valuable role in identifying systemic factors contributing to fatalities and recommending preventive measures. However, they also face challenges related to resource constraints, confidentiality concerns, biases, limited authority, and effectiveness evaluation. Addressing these limitations requires an ongoing commitment to transparency, collaboration, and evidence-based practices to ensure that fatality review teams fulfill their potential in enhancing public safety.

9

+

Policy

This chapter is presented in two parts. The first part is devoted to advocating policies for established DVDRs that operate in non-indigenous communities. Policies aimed at indigenous communities in Canada—and the United States—are presented in the second part.

PART ONE

The global and societal context in which this chapter is being written is not the same as it was when a DVDRC was first established in Ontario, Canada, an FRT in the United States, and the DHR in the United Kingdom. In 2022, the UNDOC published global estimates of female intimate partner/family-related homicides, and a "comprehensive framework" to address this problem. In 2023, and for the first time in the United States, the Biden administration launched a National Plan to End Gender-Based Violence: Strategies for Action. In the United Kingdom, Section 76 Serious Crime Act (2015) criminalized coercive controlling behavior for the first time in its history, or the history of any other country, as far as we know. A National Action Plan to Address Gender-Based Violence was created in Canada (2022).

Two significant differences between these national frameworks and strategies and DVDRs are noteworthy. One, gender-based violence is not named as the type of violence DVDRs attempt to prevent but is named in the national frameworks. Two, coercive controlling behavior is criminalized only in the United Kingdom.

On the other hand, DVDRs are the only voluntary agency in all three countries whose purposes include facilitating information exchange and coordinated interventions between hundreds of police forces and community-based organizations and agencies whose purposes include preventing family violence. This purpose is consistent with the "comprehensive approach" described in the US National Plan to end gender-based violence but not with its emphasis on intersectionality. Intersectionality draws attention to the increased risk of experiencing MPV and femicide experienced by female partners who occupy multiple statuses such as being poor, indigenous, disabled, and female. A review of DVDRs in all three countries will reveal that intersectionality is not included as a risk factor in any of them. As policy refers to "a plan of action followed by DVDRs" the plan for DVDR investigators requiring DVDR investigators to collect data on intersectionality could be included in plans for future DVDRS.

The first and perhaps most radical policy or plan would establish FRTs and DVDRCs as publicly funded independent agencies. If it is implemented, this policy would increase the likelihood that recommendations made by FRTs would not routinely reflect government policies generally, and law enforcement priorities, in particular. Moreover, publicly funded independent DVDRCs would no longer have to operate under constraints imposed by the Coroner's Act and the Freedom of Information and Privacy Act when they were located in the OCC.

The second policy would criminalize the use of designated coercive control tactics. The model for such a policy—Section 76 Serious Crimes Act—already exists in the United Kingdom. Implementing it in states in the United States and provinces in Canada would require DVDRC and FRT investigators to collect the following evidence from survivors of past attempted femicides and practitioners assessing the risk of femicide indicating:

- Partner A repeatedly or continuously engaged in behavior toward Partner B that was/is controlling or coercive;
- At the time of the behavior the two parties were personally connected;
- The behavior had a serious effect on Partner B;
- A knows or ought to know that the behavior would have a serious effect of Partner B.
- Partner B fears that violence will be carried out, and/or that,
- Serious harm or distress will be experienced leading to a substantial adverse effect on usual day-to-day activities.

Partner B and Partner A include homosexual, LGBTQ Two-Spirit, and members of other gender identity groups. A list of coercive control tactics is included in the legislation.

The third policy is aimed at settling conflicts between two worthy objectives. A conflict between the need for confidentiality and safety is present in all the DVDRs reviewed in this book. Examples include law enforcement officers being unwilling to share information that could have prevented a femicide because it may jeopardize the successful prosecution of the case; police officers serving as members of DHR advisory groups objecting to interviews with friends and relatives who could provide information relevant to prevention; the unwillingness of emergency staff in hospitals and staff in women's shelters to share information with other family violence prevention agencies.

In conducting the 2016 DHR, the panel reported conflicting demands for the need to ensure confidentiality which stands in conflict with the responsibilities of National Health Service organizations to ensure they comply with the requirements of the Duty of Candour.

The findings reported here call for a fourth policy that resolves, or at least settles the conflict by mandating information exchange between and among organizations and agencies in high-risk femicide cases identified on the basis of the results of administering the Coercive Control Scale and a field-validated risk assessment instrument.

The fifth policy is aimed at gender blindness. Gender neutrality or blindness is one of the most frequently found attributes of the DVDRs reviewed in this book. The most significant finding supporting this conclusion is the routine naming of cases where a female intentionally kills her male partner as a homicide, and also cases where a male partner kills his female partner. The latter domestic violence-related homicide case is not named a femicide in over 30 Annual Reports published DVDRs reviewed in this book over the past 20 years, and also in all the Annual Reports published by twelve different statewide FRTs in the United States and three provinces in Canada. These findings call for legislation naming a case where a male intentionally kills a female intimate partner as a family violence-related femicide, and a case where a man kills his female partner and then immediately kills himself as a suicide-femicide.

The sixth policy is grounded in findings indicating that between 30–40% of cases reviewed by DVDRs are femicide-suicide or suicide-femicide cases. Public health agency policies implemented in all three countries would require FRTs, DVDRCs, and DHRs to require the attendance of a mental health professional with police officers responding to emergency domestic violence calls.

One of the most significant sociolegal findings reported in this book is the one that DVDR recommendations have no impact on femicide. The seventh recommended policy is aimed at increasing the positive contribution DVDRs can make toward the achievement of preventing femicide and promoting system change. Such a policy would include requiring

DVDRs to (a) monitor and track recommendations, (b) reward organizations and agencies that fully implement them by increasing their funding relative to those that do not, and (c) enhance their reputations by naming them in reports submitted to the media.

The contribution made by DVDRs toward achieving their stated purposes has not, to my knowledge, ever been evaluated. Consequently, opportunities for learning lessons that could have impacted their effectiveness were lost. The eighth policy requires an independent evaluation of statewide, provincial, and large city DVDRS every five years. This is a policy recommendation that should have been implemented many years ago.

Lessons learned by suicide researchers led them to prioritize "prevention-oriented thinking and language" over prediction-oriented thinking and language because prediction is linked with suicide indirectly—suicide prevention depends upon our ability to predict it, while prevention depends upon the acquisition of knowledge on how to prevent suicide (Pisani et al., 2016). The ninth policy calls for allocating greater funding for prevention-oriented DVDRS relative to prediction-oriented DVDRs. This policy is warranted on the grounds that DVDR recommendations are more likely to make a greater contribution toward preventing family violence and femicide than prediction-oriented DVDRs.

Findings indicating that NFS significantly increases the probability of femicide (Glass et al., 2008) provides sound grounds for (a) legislation aimed at mandating the documentation of NFS by community-based healthcare practitioners using the online form published by the Training Institute on Strangulation, and (b) referral of NFS victims detected by this form to hospitals using alternative light source to detect injuries that are not revealed by sight, hearing, or touch. Effective prosecution is facilitated by the availability of information from both sources (Sharman et al., 2023). This is the tenth policy recommendation.

The National Domestic Violence publication of FAQs also included several "Policy Changes Made Because of Fatality Reviews." They were reviewed to find out whether some or all of the policy changes described here were redundant because they had already been published by this source. The review did not include any policies identified in this chapter but given the degree of cultural diversity present in the United States, Canada, and the United Kingdom, one policy included in the FAQ publication that should also be included in this book, is policy number twelve aimed at providing core funding for competent and ethnically unbiased translating services in domestic violence cases.

Another FAQ policy also addressed the topic of "decreasing the dangers posed by suicidal abusers," by calling for a protocol requiring police officers (a) to "routinely ask about the abuser's history of making homicidal or suicidal threats, and (b) urging the victim to call a domestic violence program for help with safety planning." The 12th policy recommendation calls for the replacement of (a) and (b) with the creation of a designated emergency call number (988) that requires a mental health specialist to accompany police officers responding to calls when mental illness is suspected or identified by the caller.

The relatively high degree of gender and ethnic diversity present in the United States, Canada, and the United Kingdom, plus the significance of conflict between in and out groups as an instigator of conflicts that tend to be settled by the use of violence (Weisel & Bohm, 2015), calls for a policy requiring the inclusion of teaching "healthy and respectful relationships between individuals and members of different groups" in the school curriculum. The source of policy number twelve is a recommendation made by Messing et al. (2014).

Findings revealing a strong link between firearms in the home and femicide provide robust grounds for implementing the 13th policy recommendation described below for Canada and the United States.

> Police officers attending domestic violence calls MUST (in original) seize all firearms, unless there is significant information based on the administration of a field validated risk assessment instrument that the THREAT HARM and RISK is minimal. In addition to the severity of the incident (violent crime), police officers should also consider coercive controlling behaviors and understand if the victim or disputant is in fear due to the presence of firearms.

This national policy is described by the Surrey and Sussex police forces in England. It would be supported by the Battered Women's Justice Project (2023, p. 15) in the United States which concluded that "Laws keeping guns out of the hands of abusers are associated with lower rates of intimate partner homicides." At this point, it is relevant to note the BWJP has also drawn attention to the failure of the states in the United States to enforce laws restricting the possession of firearms by persons convicted of a misdemeanor crime of domestic violence (United States Congressional Record 1996).

In Chapter 5, on practice implications, reference was made to a confidentiality-safety dilemma faced by physicians in hospital ERs that was solved by the choice of confidentiality over safety in high-risk-of-femicide cases. The 14th policy favoring safety over confidentiality is required for females experiencing MPV who visited hospital ERs one or more times during the past 12 months, and/or experienced life-threatening injuries at any time during their relationship with a male intimate partner. This policy would also require emergency ward nurses and doctors to routinely examine female victims who bring domestic violence-related physical injuries with them to the ER for indicators of NFS such as difficulty in swallowing, or breathing, loss of voice, bruising around the neck and bleeding into the skin (Sharman et al., 2023).

When the policies described in this chapter and the FAQ, and policies implemented by FRTs reporting to Attorney Generals in states in the United States, are compared, a striking but not surprising difference is revealed: FRTs located in or part of the office of Attorney Generals in states in the United States, are far more likely to increase the contribution made by agents of the criminal justice system to the prevention of family violence and femicide (e.g., Report of the Florida Attorney General's Statewide Domestic Violence Fatality Report, 2019, p. 23), than DVDRs where voices other than police officers are given equal or greater weight. The law enforcement voice is one of the most persuasive voices for legislators dependent upon their support to gain or retain their elected offices. DVDRs provide space for the voices of participants in civil society to be heard without jeopardizing collaboration with agents of the state. The 15th policy recommendation is aimed at establishing and funding DVDRs that are independent of government agencies and bureaucracies.

Finally, findings revealed by a detailed case analysis of DHRs in London, England, by Monique (2019) strongly support a 16th policy recommendation requiring training for chairs of DVDRs, information sharing by healthcare workers, especially doctors (general practitioners) and DVDRs themselves, and the inclusion of healthcare workers—including GPs—in DVDR advisory groups.

PART TWO

Facilitating reconciliation, recognition, and respect addresses the roots of the circumstances in indigenous communities requiring the establishment of DVDRCs (Truth and Reconciliation Commission of Canada, 2016). The policies identified are steps that can be taken toward achieving these socially significant objectives.

First, a policy requiring Boards of Education to include a course on settler colonialism and its historical and contemporary impact on indigenous peoples in the curriculum of high schools in Canada and the United States.

Second, completion of the online Four Seasons of Reconciliation course should be required for graduation from high schools in Canada and the United States.

Third, Reconciliation Education should be made a required course in the curriculum for teacher training in universities with faculties of education.

Fourth, federal government funding should prioritize the creation and enhancement of educational and employment opportunities for indigenous peoples, especially for those residing in rural and remote indigenous communities.

Fifth, federally funded Chair in Reconciliation Education should be established in all North American universities with faculties of education.

The major source of some of the policies referred to here is the Calls for Action published by the Truth and Reconciliation Commission of Canada (2016).

LESSON LEARNED

The policies described in this chapter are likely to make a positive contribution toward preventing MPV and coercive control only if they are implemented by the parties to whom they are addressed. The lesson from the passage of gun laws in the United States draws attention to loopholes in laws and the failure to enforce them by police forces.

Appendix
Training Resources

- **Practitioner training:** *Conducting a domestic homicide review: Online learning.* (2013). https://www.gov.uk/guidance/conducting-a-domestic-homicide-review-online-learning
- **Chair training:** Provided by Advocacy After Fatal Domestic Abuse (AAFDA). https://aafda.org.uk/training/home-office-funded-dhr-chair-training

References

Ahmad, F., Hogg-Johnson, S., Stewart, D. E., Skinner, H. A., Glazier, A. H., & Levinson, W. (2009). Computer assisted screening for intimate partner violence and control: A randomized trial. *Annals of Internal Medicine, 151*(2), 93–102.

Albers, G. (2017, June 6). Treaties with indigenous peoples in Canada. *The Canadian Encyclopedia*. Published online.

Alfano, S. (2006). Data: Conflict spurs suicide, homicide. *Homicides and Suicides: National Violent Death Reporting System, United States 2003–2004, Morbidity and Mortality Weekly Report.* CDC.

Ali, N. (2023). Domestic violence and homelessness. Canadian Observatory on Homelessness, York University. Online.

Alvarez, A. (2004). Evaluating fatality reviews. *Fatality Review Bulletin.* Paper presented at the 2004 National Conference on Domestic Violence Fatality Review, September 20–21, Delray Beach, Florida.

Anderson, D. J. (2003). The impact of subsequent violence of returning to an abusive partner. *Journal of Comparative Family Studies, 34,* 93–112.

Attorney General's Statewide Domestic Violence Fatality Review Team. (2019, June). *Faces of fatality.* Vol. 9 (June).

Avtgis, T., & Rancer, A. S. (2010). *Arguments, aggression and conflict: New directions in theory and research.* Routledge.

Auditor General of Ontario. (2019). Report on Office of the Chief Coroner and Ontario Forensic *Service.* Chapter 3, Section 3.08.

Azrael, D., Braga, A. A., & O'Brien, M. (2013). *Developing the capacity to understand and prevent homicide: A evaluation of the Milwaukee Homicide Review Commission.* US Department of Justice.

Bancroft, L. (2002). *Why does he do that: Inside the minds of angry and controlling men.* Berkeley Books.

Bandelli, D. (2017). *Femicide, gender and violence.* Palgrave Macmillan.

Banks, L., Crandall. C., Sklar, D., & Bauer, M. (2008). A comparison of intimate partner homicide to intimate partner homicide-suicide: One hundred and twenty-four New Mexico cases. *Violence Against Women*, 14(9), 1065–78.

Barker, A. (2022). *Making and breaking settler space: Five centuries of colonization in North America*. UBC Press.

Bartholomew, K., Cobb, R. J., & Dutton, D. G. (2009). Established and emerging perspectives on violence in intimate relationships. In J. Simpson & J. Dovidio (Eds.), *Handbook of personality and social psychology*, Vol. 2. APA Books.

Baskin, C. (2006). Systemic oppression, violence and healing in aboriginal families and communities. In R. Allaggia & C. Vine (Eds.), *Cruel but not unusual: Violence in Canadian families*. Wilfred Laurier University Press.

Battered Women's Justice Project. (2023). *Police seizure of firearms at scenes of domestic violence*.

Beaupre, P. (2014). *Intimate partner violence*. Statistics Canada.

Bender, A. K., & Lauritsen, J. L. (2021). Violent victimization among lesbian, gay and bisexual populations in the United States: Findings for the National Crime Victimization Survey, 2017–2018. *American Journal of Public Health*, 111(2), 318–26.

Block, C. (2000). *The Chicago women's health risk study: A collaborative research project*. Revised report. Illinois Criminal Justice Information Authority.

Bopp, M., Bopp, J., & Lane, P. (2003). *Aboriginal domestic violence in Canada*. Aboriginal Healing Foundation.

Bornstein, R. T. (2008). The complex relationship between dependency and domestic violence: Converging psychological factors and social forces. *American Psychologist*, 61(6), 595–606.

Bosch, R. (2017). Conflict escalation. *Oxford Research Encyclopedias*. doi.org/10 .1093/acrefore/9780190846626.013.62

Boughton, G. A. (2021). *Investigating investigations: A critical evaluation of the England and Wales Domestic Homicide Review (DHR) process*. Dissertation. University of South Wales, U.K.

Bourget, D., Gagne, P., & Moamai, J. (2000). Spousal homicide and suicide in Quebec. *Journal of Academic Psychiatry Law*, 28, 179–82.

Brant, J. (2020, May 1). Racial segregation of indigenous peoples in Canada. *The Canadian Encyclopedia*.

Brennan, S., & Boyce, J. (2013). Family-related murder-suicides. *Juristat*, Statistics Canada. 85-002-X.

Brittney, C. (2018). Intimate violence perpetration: Moving towards a comprehensive conceptual framework. *Partner Abuse*, 9(1), 1–29.

Brownridge, D. A. (2008). Understanding the elevated risk of partner violence against Aboriginal women: A comparison of two representative surveys of Canada. *Journal of Family Violence*, 23(5), 353–67.

Bruton, C., & Tyson, D. (2017). Leaving violent men: A study of women's experiences of separation in Victoria, Australia. *Australian & New Zealand Journal of Criminology*, 51(3), 339–54.

Bugega, L., Dawson, M., McIntyre, S-J., & Walsh, C. (2015). Domestic family violence death reviews: An international comparison. *Trauma, Violence & Abuse*, 16(2), 179–87.

Bureau of Justice Statistics. (2022). Femicide murder victims and victim offender relationship, 2021.

Burridge, T. (2020, September 16). Boeing's 'culture of concealment' to blame for 737 crashes. BBC News.

Campbell, K. M. (2007). "What was it they lost?" The impact of resource development on family violence in a northern Aboriginal community. *Journal of Ethnicity in Criminal Justice, 5*(10), 57–80.

Campbell, J. C., Glass, N., K., Laughon, K., & Bloom, T. (2007). Intimate partner homicide: Review and implications for research and policy. *Trauma, Violence & Abuse, 8*(3), 246–69.

Campbell, J. C., Webster, C., Koziol-Maclean, Block, C., Campbell, S D., Curry. M. A. et al. (2003). Risk factors for femicide in abusive relationships: Results from a multi-case control study. *American Journal of Public Health, 97*(7). PMC1447915.

Campbell, J., Rose, L., Kub. J., & Nedd, D. (1998). Voices of strength and resistance: A contextual and longitudinal analysis of women's responses to battering. *Journal of Interpersonal Violence, 13*(6), 743–62.

Canadian Broadcasting Corporation. (2021, January 17). *Mandatory reporting of choking necessary in fight against domestic violence police say.*

Canadian General Social Survey. (2014). Victimization. Statistics Canada, Ottawa, Canada.

Canadian Institute of Health. (2022). *Preventing youth suicide in First Nations.*

Canadian Institute of Health Research. (2023). *Science is better with sex and gender.* Ottawa, Canada.

Canadian Medical Protective Association. (2023). *Knowing how to balance duty of confidentiality and reporting obligations.*

Canadian National Network Cable News (2023) Investigators blame 737 MAX design and pilot error for crashes.

Canadian Parents of Murdered Children. (2020). *Health and social issue following the murder of a loved one.* Online.

Canadian Press. (2023, January). Woman killed by husband in 2019 told police of threats, Inquest hears. *Toronto Star*, A6.

Canadian Press. (2024, January 4). Mother who murdered daughter found dead. *Toronto Star*, A13.

Carter, J. (2014). Patriarchy and violence against women and girls. *Lancet*, November 20.

Cavanagh, K. (2003). Understanding women's responses to domestic violence. *Qualitative Social Work, 2*(30), 229–49.

Centers for Disease Control and Prevention. (2016). Health, United States, 2016. U.S. Department of Health and Human Services, National Center for Health Statistics, Washington, DC.

Chandler, M. J., & Lalonde, C. (1998). Cultural continuity as a hedge against suicide in Canada's First Nations. *Transcultural Psychiatry, 35*(2), 191–219.

ChatGPT. (2024). Evaluation of fatality review teams. Access online.

Chopra, J., Sambrock, L., McLoughlin, S., Randles, R., Palace, M., & Blinkhorn, V. (2022). Risk factors for intimate partner homicide in England and Wales. *Health and Social Care in the Community, 30*(5), 3086–309.

CNN Cable News Network (2019) Investigators blame 737 MAX design and pilot error for crashes.

Coates, K. (2008). *The Indian Act and the future of Aboriginal governance in Canada.* Research Paper for the National Centre for First Nations Governance.

Connolly, J., & Gordon, R. (2015). Co-victims of homicide: A systematic review of the literature. *Trauma Violence Abuse, 16*(4), 494–505.

Conroy, S. (2021) Spousal violence in Canada. *Juristat*, 1209-6393. Statistics Canada, Ottawa, Ontario, Canada.

Cook, E. A., Rowlands, J., Bracewell, K., & Boughton, G. (2023, February). Parallels in practice: Applying principles of research integrity and ethics in domestic violence fatality review. *Open Access, 38*, 1015–27.

Cooper, M., & Eaves, D. (1996) Suicide following homicide in the family. *Violence and Victims, 11*(2), 99–112.

Corrado, C., Marccuello-Servos, C., Boira, S., & Weil, S. (2016). Theories of femicide and their significance for social research. *Current Sociology, 64*(7), 975–95.

Cotter, A. (2013). *Homicide in Canada*. Statistics Canada.

Crawford, A. (2014). The trauma experienced by generations past having an effect in their descendants: Narrative and historical trauma among Inuit in Nunavut, Canada. *Transcultural Psychiatry, 51*(3), 339–69.

Cross, P. (2023, March 21). "Novel & aspirational." https://pamelacross.ca/novel -aspirational/

Dallas County Adult Intimate Partner Fatality Review Team. (2017). Case Review Report 2009–2013.

Daly, M., & Wilson, M. (1988). *Homicide*. Aldine de Gruyter.

Daly, M., Wilson, M., & Weghorst, S. J. (1982). Male sexual jealousy. *Ethology and Sociobiology, 3*, 11–27.

Davies, J. (2009). *Safety planning*. Greater Hartford Legal Aid. www.ghla.org

David, J-D., & Jaffray, B. (2022, November 21). Homicide in Canada, 2021. Statistics Canada, Ottawa, Canada.

Dawson, M. (2003). *Domestic violence death review committees: Speaking for the dead to protect the living*. Brief 1: Domestic Violence Death Review Committees.

Dawson, M. (2016). Brief 1: Domestic violence death review committees. Centre for Research and Education on Violence Against Women and Children, Guelph University, Guelph, Ontario.

Dawson, M. (2021). Domestic homicide review processes as a method of learning. In J. Devaney, C. Bradbury-Jones, R. J. Macey, C. Overlien, & S. Holt. (Eds.) *The Routledge international handbook of domestic violence and abuse*. pp. 671–84.

DeKeseredy, W. S., Dragiewicz, M., & Schwartz, M. D. (2017). *Abusive endings: Separation and divorce violence against women*. University of California Press.

Dekker, S. W. (2009). Just culture: Who gets to draw the line? *Cognition, Psychology & Work, 11*(3), 177–85.

Dempsey, A. (2023, December 15). Inside the fight for $ 120 billion: How Canada's broken treaty promise sparked a battle over mino-bimaadiziwin—the good life. *Toronto Star*, IN2.

Dennison, J. (2017). Entangled sovereignties: The Osage Nations interconnections with governmental and corporate authorities. *American Ethnologist, 44*(4), 694–96.

Dixon Transition Society. (2020, November 12). The connection between gun violence and violence against women. Burnaby, British Columbia, Canada. Access online.

Dobson, R. (2002). Medical advances mask epidemic of violence by cutting murder rate. *British Medical Journal, 325*(7365), 615.

Dobash, R. E., & Dobash, R. (1979). *Violence against wives*. Free Press.

Dobash, R. E., Dobash, R., Cavanagh, K., & Medina-Ariza, J. (2007). Lethal and non-lethal violence against intimate partners: Comparing male murderers to non-lethal abusers. *Violence Against Women, 13*, 329–53.

Dobash, R. E., Dobash, R. P., Cavanagh, K., & Lewis, R. (2000). *Changing violent men*. Sage.

Domestic Violence Action Plan. (2012). *Progress report update of the Final Report, Transforming our communities: Report from the Domestic Violence Advisory Council for the Minister Responsible for Women's Issues.*

Druscovich, M., & Caspari, M. (2023, July 20). America's deadly epidemic: *Violence Against Women*. Reuters.

Dugan, I., Nagin, D. S., & Rosenfeld, R. (2003). Exposure reduction or retaliation? The effects of domestic violence resources on intimate partner homicide. *Law and Society Review, 37*, 169–98.

Eckhardt, C. I., Murphy, C. M., Whitaker, D. J., Springer, L. L., Dykstra, R., & Woodard, K. (2013). The effectiveness of intervention programs for perpetrators and victims of intimate partner violence. *Partner Abuse, 4*(2), 196–230.

Edouard-Notredame, C., Devanstoy, S. D. Lesage, A., & Seguin, M. (2018). Can we discriminate homicide-suicides and suicides from their risk factors? *Criminologie, 51*(2), 314–42.

Ellis, D. (2017). Marital separation and lethal male partner violence. *Violence Against Women, 23*(4), 503–19.

Ellis, D., & Anderson, D. (2005). *Conflict resolution: An introductory text*. Emond-Montgmery.

Ellis, D., Stuckless, N., & Smith, C. (2015). *Marital separation and lethal domestic violence*. Routledge.

Elson, P., & Carmichael, P. (2022, April 12). A short history of voluntary sector-government relations in Canada (revisited). *The Philanthropist Journal*, 1–48.

Everytown Research and Policy. (2024). Guns and violence against women; America's uniquely lethal intimate partner violence problem. A program of Everytown for Gun Safety Fund. Access online.

Faure, G. O., & Sjostedt, G. (1993). Culture and negotiation: An introduction. In G. O. Faure & J. Z. Rubin (Eds.), *Culture and negotiation: The resolution of water disputes*. Sage.

Filice, M. (2016, August 2). Numbered treaties. *The Canadian Encyclopedia*. Published online.

Fisher, R., & Ury, W. (1972). *Getting to yes*. Penguin.

Fleury, R. E., Sulivan, C. E., & Bybee, D. I. (2000). When ending the relationship doesn't end the violence: Women's experiences of violence by former partners. *Violence Against Women, 6*(12), 1363–83.

Florida Violence Review Team Report. (2019, June). *Faces of fatality.*

Ford, C., & Harawan, N. T. (2010) A new conceptualization of ethnicity for social and epidemiological equity research. *Social Science Medicine, 71*(2), 251–58.

French, K. A., & Fletcher, K. (2023). Officer-involved domestic violence: A call for action among I-O psychologists. *Industrial and Organizational Psychology: Perspectives on science and practice, 15*(4), 604–608.

Fugate, M., Landis, L., Riordan, K., Naureckas, S., & Engel, B. (2005). Barriers to domestic violence help seeking: Implications for intervention. *Violence Against Women, 11*(3), 290–310.

Gallup Poll. (2024). LGBTQ+ identification in the U.S. now at 7.6%.

Garner, J. H., & Maxwell, C. D. (2009). Coordinated community response to intimate partner violence in the 20th and 21st centuries. *Criminology and Public Policy, 7*(4), 525–53.

Gavigan, S. (2013). Something old, something new? Re-theorizing patriarchal relations and privatization from the outskirts of family law. *Theoretical Inquiries in Law, 13*(1), 271–301.

Gillis, W., & Hasham, A. (2017, January 9). When men kill their partners, warning signs often missed. *Toronto Star.*

Glass, N., Laughton, K., Campbell, J., Block, C. R., Hanson, G., Sharps, P. W., & Taliaferro, E. (2008). Non-fatal strangulation is an important risk factor for homicide of women. *Journal of Emergency Medicine, 35*(30), 329–35.

Global Social Theory. (2016). Settler colonialism. Covered by Creative Commons License. Web Page CC BY-NVC-ND 3.0.

Goode, W. J. (1971, November). Force and violence in the family. *Journal of Marriage and the Family,* 624–35.

Goodkind, J. R., Sullivan, C. M., & Bybee, D. I. (2004). A contextual analysis of battered women's safety planning. *Violence Against Women, 10*(5), 511–33.

Goodman, L., Dutton, M. A., Vankos, N., & Weinfurt, K. (2005). Women's resources and use of strategies as risk and protective factors for re-abuse over time. *Violence Against Women, 11*(3), 311–36.

Goodmark, L. (2004). Law is the answer? How do we know that for sure? Questioning the efficacy of legal interventions for battered women. *Saint Louis Public Law Review, 23*(7), 1–44.

Goodmark, L. (2007). Going underground: The ethics of advising battered women fleeing an abusive relationship. *75 UMKC Law Review,* 999–1023.

Gottman, J. M., Murray, J. D., Swanson, C. C., Tyson, R., & Swanson, K. R. (2002). *The mathematics of marriage: Dynamic non-linear models.* MIT Press.

Government of Canada. (2019). *Reclaiming power and place: The final report of the National Inquiry into missing and murdered indigenous women and girls.*

Government of Canada. (2021). *Making the links in family violence cases: Collaboration among the family, child protection and criminal justice systems.* Department of Justice.

Government of Canada. (2022). *Terms of reference: Indigenous Advisory Committee Circle of Experts Sub-Committee.* Impact Assessment Agency of Canada.

Graham-Kevan, N., & Archer, J. (2008). Does controlling behavior predict physical aggression and violence to partners. *Journal of Family Violence, 23,* 539–48.

Graham, L. M., Macy, R. G., Rizo, C. F., & Martin, S. L. (2022). Explanatory theories of intimate partner homicide perpetration: A systematic review. *Trauma Violence Abuse, 23*(2), 408–27.

Greenspun, D. (2005). *Woman abuse: Screening, identification and initial response.* Registered Nurses Association of Ontario.

Gross, B. (2007) Life sentence: Co-victims of homicide. *Annals of the American Psychotherapy Association, 10*(3), 39.

Hamilton, W. D. (1964). The genetic evolution of social behavior. *Journal of Theoretical Biology, 7,* 1–52.

Hart, B. (2015). *Rule making and rule enforcement: The violent and controlling tactics of men who batter.* Washington State Coalition Against Domestic Violence.

Hauser, J. (2005). Commentary on Websdale. *Violence Against Women, 11*(9), 1202–205.

Hayes, M. (2023, August 16). Intimate partner violence an 'epidemic', federal government says in response to coroner's inquest. *The Globe and Mail*.

Heidinger, L. (2022). Violent victimization and perceptions of safety: Experiences of First Nations, Metis and Inuit women in Canada. *Juristat*, 2022001. Statistics Canada, Ottawa.

Heise, L. (1998). Violence against women: An integrated ecological framework. *Violence Against Women*, 4(3), 262–90.

Heise, L. (2011). *What works to prevent partner violence: An evidence overview*. Strive Research Consortium. Centre for Gender Violence and Health London School of Hygiene and Tropical Medicine. London. Funded by the Policy Division of the UK Department for International Development.

Heron, R. L., & Eisma, M. C. (2021). Barriers and facilitators of disclosing domestic violence: A systematic review of qualitative research. *Health Care Community*, 29, 612–30.

Holmes, C., & Hunt, S. (2017). *Indigenous communities and family violence: Changing the conversation*. National Collaboration Centre for Aboriginal Health, Prince George, B.C. Canada. www.nccah.ca.

Holmes, J. L., & Backes, B. (2016). *The Domestic Violence Homicide Prevention Demonstration Initiative*. Department of Justice.

Home Office. (2006a). *Domestic homicide reviews: Key findings from the analysis of domestic homicide reviews*.

Home Office. (2006b). *DHR Guidance under the Domestic Violence Crime and Victims Act*.

Home Office. (2016). *Multi-agency statutory guidelines for the conduct of homicide reviews*.

Hoyle, C. (2008). Will she be safe? A critical analysis of risk assessment in domestic violence cases. *Children and Youth Services Review*, 30, 323–37.

Humphrey, P. S. (1980). Offender-victim relationships in criminal homicide followed by offender's suicide, North Carolina, 1972–1977. *Suicide and Life Threatening Behavior*, 10(2), 106–18.

Hunnicutt, G. (2009). Varieties of patriarchy and violence against women: resurrecting "patriarchy" as a theoretical tool. *Violence Against Women*, 15(5), 553–73.

Hussain N., Sprague, S., Madden, K., Naz Hussain, F Pindiprolu, B., & Bhandari, M. (2015). A comparison of types of screening tool administration methods used for the detection of intimate partner violence: A systematic review and meta-analysis. *Trauma, Violence, & Abuse*, 16(1), 60–69.

Indigenous Services Canada. (2020). Annual Report to Parliament. Canada.ca.

Irving, L., & Chi-Pun Liu, B. (2020). Beaten into submissiveness? An investigation into the protective strategies used by survivors of domestic abuse. *Journal of Interpersonal Violence*, 35(1–2), 294–318.

Jaffee, P., Dawson, M., & Campbell, C. (2008, October 20–21). *Multidisciplinary perspectives on preventing domestic homicides: A discussion paper from a Canadian think-tank*. Domestic Violence Death Review Committee, Toronto.

Johnson, H. (2012). When feminism meets evolutionary psychology: The enduring legacy of Margo Wilson. *Homicide Studies*, 16(4), 332–45.

Johnson, H., Eriksson, L., & Wortley, R. (2019). Intimate femicide: The role of coercive control. *Feminist Criminology*, 14, 3–23.

Johnson, H., & Hotton, T. (2003). Losing control: Homicide risk in estranged and intact intimate relationships. *Homicide Studies, 7,* 58–84.

Johnson, J. N., Richardson, C., Dawson, M., Campbell, M., Bader, D., Fairbairn, J., Straatman, A. L., Poon, J., & Jaffee, P. (2019). *Domestic violence and homicide in rural, remote and northern communities: Understanding risk and keeping women safe.* Canadian Domestic Violence Prevention Initiative. Centre for the Study of Legal and Social Responses to Violence. University of Guelph, Ontario.

Johnson, P. (1983). *Native children and the child welfare system.* Report prepared for the Canadian Council on Social Development. James Lorimer and Co.

Jones, C., Bracewell, K., Clegg., A. Stanley, N., & Chantler, K. (2022). Domestic homicide review committees' recommendations and impacts: A systematic review. *Homicide Studies, 28*(1), 78–98.

Just Facts. (2023). Victimization of indigenous women and girls. Research and Statistics Division, Department of Justice, Government of Canada, Ottawa.

Kafka, J. M., Moracco, K., Taheri, C.., Rose-Young, B., Graham, L. M., Macy, R. J., & Proescholdbell, S. (2019). Intimate partner violence victimization and perpetration as precursors to suicide. *SSM Population Health* (2022). Covered under a Creative Commons License.doi.org/10.1016/j.ssmph.2022.101079/.

Kelly, J. B., & Johnson, M. P. (2008). Differentiation among types of intimate partner violence: Research update and implications for intervention. *Family Court Review, 46*(33), 476–99.

Kirkwood, C. (1993). *Leaving abusive partners.* Sage.

Kopp, R. T., & Mannitz, S. (2022). Approaches to decolonizing settler colonialism: Examples from Canada. Working Papers, # 58. *Truth and Reconciliation Commission of Canada.*

Kuennen, T. (2013). "Struck on love." *Denver University Law Review,* 171, 1–10.

Li, F., & Chen, C. (2023). Should the time interval be defined in homicide-suicide cases? *Creative Commons.* doi.org/10.21203/rs-2589418/v1

Liem, M. (2010). Homicide-parasuicide: A qualitative comparison with homicide and para-suicide. *Journal of Forensic Psychiatry and Psychology, 21,* 247–63.

Liem, M., & Nieuwbeerta, P. (2010). Homicide followed by suicide: A comparison with homicide and suicide. *Suicide and Life-Threatening Behavior, 40,* 133–45.

Lindsay, M. (2014). *Violence perpetrated by ex-spouses in Canada.* Research and Statistics Division, Department of Justice, Canada.

Long, J., Wertans, W. E., Harper, K., Brennan, D., Harvey, H., Allen, R., & Elliott, K. (2020). *Femicide Census: UK Femicides 2009–2018.* Report prepared for the Edith Eligator and Treebeard Trust, Cambridge, England.

Los Angeles Times Editorial Board. (2022, April 14). Editorial: Sheriffs shouldn't be coroners too: Split the job. *Los Angeles Times.*

Mahoney, M. (1991). Redefining the issue of separation. *Michigan Law Review, 90,* 1–94.

Markham, H. (1993). *We can work it out: Making sense of marital conflict.* Putnam.

Marzuk, P. M., Tardiff, K., & Hirsch, C. S. (1992). The epidemiology of murder-suicide. *Journal of the American Medical Association, 267,* 3179–83.

Mason, A., & Cross, P. (2022). Why femicide inquests are important. Dawson Women's Shelter. https://dawsonwomensshelter.com/blog/femicide-inquests.

McHardy, L. W., & Hofford, M. (1999). *Fatality reviews: Recommendations from a national summit.* Office of Justice Programs, US Department of Justice.

Mennicke, A. M., & Ropes, K. (2016). Estimating the risk of domestic violence by law enforcement officers: A review of methods and estimates: *Aggression and Violent Behavior, 31*, 157–64.

Mercy, J. A., Hillis, S. D., Butchart, A., Bellis, M. A., Ward, C. L., Fang, X., & Rosenberg, M. L. (2017). Interpersonal violence: Global impact and paths to prevention. In N. R. Mock & O. Kobusingye, *Injury prevention and environment health.* 3rd ed. International Bank for Reconstruction and Development & The World Bank.

Messing, J. T., Campbell, J., Wilson, J. S., Brown, S., Patchell, B., & Shall, B. (2014). *Police departments' use of the Lethality Assessment Program: A quasi-experimental evaluation.* Department of Justice.

Miller, A. G. (1994). Culture and everyday social explanations. *Journal of Experimental and Social Psychology, 3*(1), 961–78.

Moncton-Smith, J. (2020). Intimate partner femicide: Using Foucauldian analysis to track an eight-stage relationship progression to homicide. *Violence Against Women, 26*(11), 1267–1285.

Moncton-Smith, J. (2021, February 21). Domestic abuse isn't in a row: It's when one person has become a threat to another. Interview with Andrew Anthony. *The Guardian.*

Monique, B. (2019). *London Domestic Homicide Review: Case analysis and review of local authorities DHR process.* Report published for the Mayor of London and Standing Together.

Montanez, J., Donley, A., & Reckenwald, A. (2020, July). Intersecting dimensions of violence, abuse and victimization.

Morton, W. (2014). *Northern Territory domestic and family violence reduction strategy.* National Northern Territory Council of Social Services.

Mosleh, O. (2024). Couple's death rattles community. *Toronto Star*, A3.

Murray, J., Farrington, D. P., & Eisner, E. P. (2009). Drawing conclusions about causes from systematic reviews of risk factors: The Cambridge Quality Checklists. *Journal of Experimental Criminology, 5*, 1–23.

Musielak, N., Jaffe, P., & Lapshina, J. (2020). Barriers to safety for victims of domestic homicide. *Psychology, Crime and Law, 26*, 461–78.

Myhill, A., & Hohl, K. (2016). The "golden thread": coercive control and risk assessment for domestic violence. *Journal of Interpersonal Violence, 34*(21–22), 4477–97.

Nagy, R., & Sehdev, R. K. (2023). *Introduction: Residential schools and decolonization.* Cambridge University Press.

National Action Plan (2024). Government of Canada, Ottawa, Ontario, Canada.

National Archive of Criminal Justice. (2015). ICPSC—Interuniversity for social and political research. *Criminal Justice Review (2001), 26*(2), 193–208.

National Council of Juvenile and Family Court Judges. (1999). Effective intervention in domestic violence and child mistreatment cases: Guidelines for policy and practice. Reno, Nevada

National Fatality Review Initiative. (2024, March). Active review team in all but six states in the U.S. Access Online.

National Network to End Domestic Violence. (n.d.). Frequently asked questions about domestic violence.

National Resource Center on Domestic Violence. (2021). *Addressing root causes.* VAWnet.

Nease, K. (2022, October 4). Big changes could be coming to the domestic killings review committee. *CBC News*.

Nicolaidis, C., Curry, M. A., Ulrich, Y., Sharps, P., McFarlane, J., Campbell, D., Gary, F., Laughon, K., Glass, N., & Campbell, J. (2003). Could we have known? A qualitative analysis of data from women who survived an attempted homicide by an intimate partner. *Journal of General Internal Medicine, 18*, 788–94.

Niolan, P. H. et al. (2017). *Preventing intimate partner violence across the lifespan: A technical package of programs, policies and practices*. Division of Violence Prevention and Control, Centers for Disease Control and Prevention.

Onishi, N. (2023, June 4). In a power struggle over the Arctic, Canada turns to those who know it best. *New York Times*, pp. 1, 18.

Ontario Medical Students Association. (2023). Tackling the increasing public health impact of firearms: A call for action. Position paper (May). Access online.

Orange, T. (2019). Where the dead sit talking. *University of Nebraska Press, 31*(1–2), 237-254.

Orange, T. (2024). *Wandering stars*. Penguin Random House.

Ornstein, P., & Rickne, J. (2013). When does intimate partner violence continue after separation? *Violence Against Women, 19*(95), 617–33.

Palermo, G. (1994). Murder-suicide: An extended suicide. *International Journal of Offender Therapy and Comparative Criminology, 31*, 205–16.

Paradies, Y. (2016). Colonisation, racism and indigenous health. *Journal of Population Research, 33*, 83–96.

Peled, E., Eisikovits, Z., & Winstock, Z. (2000). Choice and empowerment for battered women who stay: Toward a constructivist model. *Social Work, 45*(10), 1–26.

Pence, E., & Paymar, M. (1993). *Education groups for men who batter: The Duluth Model*. Springer.

Penfold, R. B. (2005). *Dragonslippers: This is what an abusive relationship really looks like*. Penguin.

Petrosky, E., Kollar, L. M., Kearns, M. C., Smith, S. G., Betz, C. J., Fowler, K. A., & Satter, D. E. (2021). Homicides of American Indians/Alaska Natives—National Violent Death Reporting System, United States, 2003-2018.

Pisani, A., Murrie, D., & Silverman, M. (2016). *Academic Psychiatry, 40*, 623–29.

Pizzaro, J. M., & Zeoli, A. (2011). An assessment of the quality of homicide data in Supplementary Homicide Reports: A research note. *Justice Quarterly, 30*(4), 1–21.

Pobutsky, A., Brown, M., Nakao, L., & Reyes-Salvail, F. (2014). Results from the Hawaii domestic violence fatality review, 2000–2009. *Journal of Violence Injury Research, 6*(2), 79–90.

Polk, K. K. (1994). *When men kill*. Cambridge University Press.

Pow, A. M., Murray, C. E., Flasch, P., Doom, E., & Snyder, M. (2015). Learning from experience: A content analysis of domestic violence fatality review team reports. *Partner Abuse, 6*, 197–216.

Pronyk, P. M. et al. (2022). Effect of a structural intervention for the prevention of intimate partner violence and HIV in rural South Africa; A cluster randomised trial. *The Lancet, 368*(9581), 11073–983.

Pruitt, D. G., & Rubin, J. Z. (1986). *Social conflict: Escalation, stalemate and settlement*. Random House.

Radford, J. (2019). *Femicide Census: UK Femicides 2009–2018*. In K. I. Smith & C. O'Callaghan, p. 14. Report funded by Edith Eligator and Treebeard Trust, Cambridge, England.

Regoeczi, W. C., & Gilson, T. (2018). Homicide-suicide in Cuyahoga County, Ohio. *Journal of Forensic Psychiatry and Psychology, 63*(5), 1539–44.

Renker, P. R. (2008). Breaking the barriers: The promise of computer-assisted screening for intimate partner violence. *Journal of Midwifery & Women's Health, 53*(6), 496–502.

Rezey, M. L. (2017). Separated women's risk for intimate partner violence: A multi-year analysis using the National Crime Victimization Survey. *Journal of Interpersonal Violence, 35*, 1055–80.

Rheault, D. (2011) Solving the Indian problem: Assimilation laws, practices and Indian residential schools. Metis Professor, Fleming College, Peterborough, Ontario, Canada.

Robinson, A. L., Rees, A., & Dehaghani, R. (2019). Making connections: A multi-disciplinary analysis of domestic homicide, mental health homicide and adult practice reviews. *Journal of Adult Protection, 21*(1), 16–26.

Roehl, J., & Guertin, K. (2000). Intimate partner violence: The current use of risk assessment in screening offenders. *The Justice System Journal, 21*(2), 171–98.

Rosay, A. B. (2016, June 1). Violence against American Indian and Alaskan women. *National Institute of Justice Journal.*

Rosenfeld, D. J. (2022). The high-risk team model and GPS offender monitoring: Stopping DV in its tracks. *Domestic Violence Report, 17*(30), 33–46.

Rowlands, D. J., & Bracewell, K. (2022). Inside the black box: Domestic reviews as a source of data. *Journal of Gender-Based Violence, 6*(30), 518–34.

Royal Commission on Aboriginal Peoples. (1996). Gathering Strength (Vol. 3). *Report of the Royal Commission on Aboriginal Peoples.*

Rubenstein, C. (2004). Listening for a change. Paper presented at the National Conference on Domestic Violence fatality reviews, September 20–21, Delray Beach, Florida.

Saint-Germain, B. (2022). *Canadian history: Indigenous peoples.* University of Victoriata.

Sampson, F. (2003). The coroner's inquest as an equality rights mechanism: A case study of the May-Iles Coroner's inquest into domestic violence in Ontario. *Journal of Law and Social Policy, 18*, 75–97.

Santana, V. S., Filho, N., de Aimedia., da Rocha, C. O., & Matos, A. S. (1997). Proxy informant reliability and bias in epidemiological research: Analysis of a screening questionnaire for mental disorders. *Rev Saude Publica, 31*(6), 556–65.

Saxton, M. D., Jaffee, P. G., & Olszowy, R. (2020). The police role in domestic homicide prevention: Lessons from a domestic violence death review committee. *Journal of Interpersonal Violence, 37*(3–4), 1886-1.

Sharman, L. S., Douglas, H. & Fitzgerald, R. (2023). Medical evidence assisting non-fatal strangulation: A scoping review. *British Medical Journal, 13*, 1–11.

Sharp-Jeffs, N., Kelly, L., & Klein, R. (2018). Long journeys towards freedom: The relationship between coercive control and space for action-measurement and emerging evidence. *Violence Against Women, 24*(2), 163–85.

Shiva, V. (1997). *Biopiracy: The plunder of nature and knowledge.* South End.

Silver, N. (2012). *The signal and the noise.* Penguin.

Singhai S., Orr, S., Singh, H., Shanmuganantha, M., & Manson, H. (2021). Domestic violence related emergency room visits in Ontario, Canada. *BMC Public Health, 21*, 1–9.

Sinha, M. (2013). *Intimate partner violence.* Statistics Canada.

Sorrentino, A., Cinquegrana, V., & Guida, C. (2022). Risk factors for intimate partner femicide in Italy: An ecological approach. *International Journal of Environmental Research and Public Health, 19*, 1–14.

Sowan, W. (2023). A conflict escalation comparison: couples from the general population and couples engaged in high-intensity conflict. In W. Sowan, *Family Relations.* Wiley, on behalf of the National Council on Family Relations.

SpearChief-Morris, J. (2024a, May 11). PM to name commissioner for Indigenous treaties. *Toronto Star*, A11.

SpearChief-Morris, J. (2024b, May 2). Ottawa commits $187 million to 'shed colonial habits.' *Toronto Star*, A9.

Spiwak, R., & Brownridge, D. A. (2005). Separated women's risk for violence: An analysis of the Canadian Situation. *Journal of Divorce and Remarriage, 43*(3/4), 105–17.

Standing Together. (2021). *What is a community coordinated response?* standing together.org.uk

Starblanket, G. (2019). The Numbered Treaties and the politics of incoherency. *Canadian Journal of Political Science, 52*(93), 443–59.

Stark, E., & Hester, M. (2018). Coercive control: Update and review. *Violence Against Women, 25*, 81–104.

Statistics Canada (2023) Trends in police reported family violence and intimate partner homicide. Canadian Centre for Justice and Community Safety, Ottawa, Canada.

Statistics Canada (2016). Indigenous foster children living in private households: Rates and household characteristics. *The Daily*, Ottawa.

Statistics Canada. (2018). *Report on the prevalence of homicide across Canada.* Ottawa, Canada.

Statistics Canada (2018b). Report on the prevalence of homicide across Canada. Ottawa, Ontario.

Statistics Canada. (2019a). *Homicide in Canada.*

Statistics Canada. (2019b). *Suicide among First Nations people, Metis and Inuit.*

Statistics Canada. (2022). *Estimates of population as of July 1st, by marital status or legal marital status, age and sex.* doi.org/10.25318/1710006001-eng.

Stets, J. (1988). *Domestic violence and conrol.* Springer.

Storer, H. L., Lindhorst, T., & Kelly, S. (2013). The domestic fatality review: Can it mobilize community level change? *Homicide Studies, 17*(4), 418–35.

Stout, K. (1992). Intimate femicide: An ecological analysis. *The Journal of Sociology and Social Welfare, 19*(3), 29–50.

Straus, M. A. (1979). Measuring intra family conflict and violence: The Conflict Tactics Scales.*Journal of Marriage and the Family, 41*(1), 75–88.

Straus, M., & Gelles, R. J. (1990). *Physical violence in American families: Risk factors and adaptations to violence in 8,145 families.* Transaction Publishers.

Supreme Court of Canada. (1999). R v Gladue CanLII 679 CSCC.

Sutton, D. (2023). *Gender-related homicides of women and girls in Canada.* Statistics Canada, Ottawa.

Tait, P. I. (2007). *Systems of conflict resolution within First Nations communities.* Honouring the Elders, Honouring the Knowledge. Research paper for the National Centre for First Nations Governance.

Tannen, D. (1998). *The argument culture.* Barnes and Noble.

Taylor, R., & Jasinski, J. (2011). Femicide and the femicide perspective. *Homicide Studies, 15*(4), 341–62.

The Daily. (2022). *Violent victimization and perceptions of safety among First Nations, Metis and Inuit Women and among women living in remote areas of Canada.* Jursitsat, Statistics Canada.

Thibaut, J. W., & Kelley, H. H. (1985). *The social psychology of groups.* Wiley.

Thornton, S. (2017). Police attempts to predict domestic murder and serious assaults: Is early warning possible yet? *Cambridge Journal of Evidence-Based Policing, 1,* 64–80.

Tjaden, P., & Thoennes, N. (2000) Prevalence and consequences of male-to-female intimate partner violence as measured by the National Violence Against Women Survey. *Family Court Review, 6,* 142–61.

Towns, A., & Adams, P. (2000). "If I really loved him enough, he would be okay." *Violence Against Women, 6*(60), 558–85.

Truth and Reconciliation Commission of Canada. (2016). *Canada's Residential Schools: The Inuit and Northern Experience,* Vol. 2. McGill-Queens University Press.

Turner, E., Medina, J., & Brown, G. (2019). Dashing hopes? The predictive accuracy of domestic abuse risk assessment instruments. *The British Journal of Criminology, 59*(5), 1013–34.

United Nations. (2022, March 22). *Violence against women, girls may be the world's longest, deadliest pandemic.* Address by Secretary General to Group of Friends Commission Event.

United States Congressional Record. (1996). Restrictions on the Possession of Firearms by Individuals Convicted of a Misdemeanor Crime of Domestic Violence. Washington, D.C.

UNODC. United Nations Office of Drugs and Crime. (2022). *Gender-related killings of women and girls (femicide).* Vienna, Austria. UNODC-ddds@un.org

UNODC. United Nations Office of Drugs and Crime. (2023). *Background paper on femicide review committees.* Commission on Crime Prevention and Criminal Justice. 33rd session. Vienna, May 22–26.

Vallee, B. (1998). *Life and death with Billy.* Seal Books.

Van Kirk, S. (1984). The role of native women in the fur trade society of Western Canada, 1670-1830. *Women on the Western Frontier, 7*(3), 9-13.

Violence Policy Center. (2021). *When men murder women: An analysis of 2021 homicide data.* National Resource Center on gender-based violence.

Visher, C. A., Harralell, A., Newmark, L., & Yahner, J. (2008). Reducing intimate partner violence: A evaluation of a comprehensive justice system-community collaboration. *Criminology & Public Policy, 4,* 495–523.

Walby, S. (1990). *Theorising patriarchy.* Basil Blackwell.

Waldman, M. C., & Muelleman, R. L. (1999). Domestic violence homicides: ED use before victimization. *American Journal of Emergency Medicine, 17*(7), 689–91.

Walker, M., McGlade, M., & Gamble, J. (2008). A domestic homicide review of the deaths of Julia and William Pemberton. Online access.

Watt, K. A. (2010). *Domestic violence fatality review teams: Collaborative efforts to prevent intimate partner femicide.* Dissertation, University of Illinois at Urbana-Champaign.

Websdale, N. (2003, November). Reviewing domestic violence deaths. *NIJ Journal*, 250, 26–31.

Websdale, N. (2019). The Montana Native American domestic violence fatality review team. 11(3), 31–38.

Websdale, N. (2020). Domestic violence fatality review: The state of the art. In R. Geffner et al. (Eds.), *Handbook of interpersonal violence and abuse across the lifespan.* pp. 121–23.

Websdale, N., Sheeran, M., & Johnson, B (2001) Reviewing domestic violence fatalities: Summarizing national developments. Minnesota Center Against Violence and Abuse, Minneapolis.

Websdale, N., Ferraro, K., & Barger, S. D. (2019). The domestic violence fatality review clearinghouse: Introduction to a new National Data System with a focus on firearms. *Injury Epidemiology, 6*(6), 1–14.

Websdale, N., Town, M., & Johnson, B. (1999). Domestic fatality reviews: From a culture of blame to a culture of safety. In M. Town & B. Johnson (Eds.), *Problem solving courts, restorative justice, therapeutic justice.*

Weisel, O., & Bohm, R. (2015). "In-group love" and "out-group hate' in intergroup conflict between natural groups. *Journal of Experimental Social Psychology, 60*, 110–20.

West, D. J. (1965). *Murder followed by suicide.* Harvard University Press.

Wetendorf, D. (2021). *Crossing the threshold: Female officers and police perpetrated domestic violence.* Books2Read.

Wilson, M., & Daly, M. (1992). Till death do us part. In J. Radford & D. E. Russell (Eds.), *Femicide: The politics of woman killing.* Twane.

Winstock, Z., & Eisikovits, Z. (2008). Motives and control in escalatory conflicts in intimate relationships. *Children and Youth Services, 30*, 287–96.

Wolfe, P. (2006) Settler colonialism and the elimination of the native. *Journal of Genocide Research, 8*(4), 387-409.

Woods, A. (2023, March 31). Shooter's spouse screen as 'first victim.' *Toronto Star*, A9.

Women and Gender Equality Canada. (2023). *The Government of Canada and Nunavut sign two bilateral agreements to end gender-based violence.*

World Health Organization. (2020). Homicide: Global Health Estimates (2019 update).

Zahn, M. A. (2003) Intimate partner homicide: An overview. *National Institute of Justice Journal*, 250. US Department of Justice, National Institute of Justice.

Zeoli, A. M., Malinski, R., & Brenner, H. (2020). The intersection of firearms and intimate partner homicide. *Trauma, Abuse & Violence, 4*, 45–56.

Zeppegno, P., Gramaglia, C., de Marco, S., Guerriero, C., Consol, C., Loreti, L., Martelli, M., Maraangon, D., Carli, V., & Sarchiapone, M. (2019). Intimate partner homicide-suicide: A mini-review of the literature (2012–2018).*Current Psychology Reports, 21*, 11–17.

Zinov, H. M., Rheingold, A. A., Hawkins, A. O, Saunders, B. E., & Kilpatrick, D. G. (2009). Losing a loved one to homicide: Prevalence and mental health correlates in a national sample of young adults. *Journal of Trauma Stress, 22*(910), 20–27.

Index

173

About the Author

Desmond Ellis is a Professor Emeritus based in the La Marsh Centre for Child and Youth Research, Faculty of Health, York University. During his tenure at York, he was appointed to the Domestic Violence Subcommittee to the Federal U.S. Uniform Collaborative Law Act Task Force and the Advisory Committee, Family Mediation Service, Superior Court of Justice, Toronto. He also served as a Board member for Conflict Mediation Services, Downsview, Ontario, published several research reports, books, and articles on separation and divorce mediation, and created the La Marsh Centre on Violence and Conflict Resolution and the Certificate Program in Dispute Resolution. His most recent book, *Domestic Violence: A Practical Handbook for Family Lawyers*, was published by Lexis-Nexis in 2019. He has been appointed by Justice Canada to the Family Violence Advisory Group to implement national family violence user guidelines for family violence practitioners to identify and respond to family violence.

www.ingramcontent.com/pod-product-compliance
Lightning Source LLC
Chambersburg PA
CBHW031135270326
41929CB00011B/1638